DAVID

ESSA

WRITERS SERIES 16

ANTONIO D'ALFONSO AND JOSEPH PIVATO

Guernica Editions Inc. acknowledges the support of
The Canada Council for the Arts and the Ontario Arts Council.

DAVID ADAMS RICHARDS

ESSAYS ON HIS WORKS

EDITED BY TONY TREMBLAY

GUERNICA

TORONTO · BUFFALO · CHICAGO · LANCASTER (U.K.)

2005

Copyright © 2005, by Tony Tremblay, the Authors,
and Guernica Editions Inc.
All rights reserved. The use of any part of this publication, reproduced,
transmitted in any form or by any means, electronic, mechanical,
photocopying, recording or otherwise stored in a retrieval system, without
the prior consent of the publisher is an infringement of the copyright law.

Tony Tremblay, Guest Editor
Guernica Editions Inc.
P.O. Box 117, Station P, Toronto (ON), Canada M5S 2S6
2250 Military Road, Tonawanda, N.Y. 14150-6000 U.S.A.

Distributors:
University of Toronto Press Distribution,
5201 Dufferin Street, Toronto (ON), Canada M3H 5T8
Gazelle Book Services, White Cross Mills, High Town,
Lancaster LA1 1XS U.K.
Independent Publishers Group,
814 N. Franklin Street, Chicago, Il. 60610 U.S.A.

First edition.
Printed in Canada.
Legal Deposit — Second Quarter
National Library of Canada
Library of Congress Catalog Card Number: 2004101875
National Library of Canada Cataloguing in Publication
David Adams Richards : essays on his works / edited by Tony Tremblay.
(Writers series ; 16)
ISBN 1-55071-199-7

1. Richards, David Adams. — Criticism and interpretation.
I. Tremblay, M. Anthony (Michael Anthony).
II. Series: Writers series (Toronto, Ont.) ; 16.
PS8585.I17Z63 2004   C813'.54   C2004-901101-4

Contents

Acknowledgements

Most of the essays in this collection have been reprinted, with permission of the authors, from a special issue of *Pottersfield Portfolio* on David Adams Richards 19.1 (Fall 1998): 5-80.

"David Adams Richards: Canada's Independent Intellectual" by Tony Tremblay is reprinted from *The Hollins Critic* 36.4 (October 1999): 1-14.

Introduction

Richards Among His Readers

TONY TREMBLAY

The relationship between artists and critics is complex – sometimes symbiotic, sometimes parasitic. Perspective, as always, is everything. Most critics like to think of their interactions with artists as symbiotic, many artists think of critics as parasites. Personally, I prefer Anatole France's critic (who "tells of his mind's adventures among masterpieces") to Henry James's (who is "the real helper of the artist, a torchbearing outrider, the interpreter, the brother"). James's critic, it seems to me, extracts too much of a take in what the artist has made. And if the take is lofty so is it assumed that the critic's pronouncements are equal to (even superior to) the work of art. Investment and return tend to work like that. However, to value the critic over the artist is to selfishly accept the liberties of modern permissiveness, placing the practice of scholarship and the institution of the academy over the act of creation. If that sounds theoretically naive, then so be it, but the culture that results from placing scholarship above art is one that is often hostile to all but the artists it has chosen to represent it. That we live in such a culture, though shocking to contemplate, should be no surprise. On the strength of our institutionalizing fervour, we have become a culture of critics, openly hostile to artists. In Wyndham Lewis's phrase, we have become "men without art." That artists of the sensibility of David Adams Richards have come to spurn critics (a waste of creative energy, in my view) is proof positive of the insidiousness of this permissive license.

My own interest in David Adams Richards' work is two-fold, involving first and most importantly his sense of my place (he has rendered the world I come from artistically, evoking its rhythms exactly) and, second, his rough handling by establishment critics, those who have sought to discredit him. Where I come from a snub from an outsider against one of your own – never mind that he is a towering artistic talent – is an instant formula for friendship, and so it was that I befriended David Richards (and ten years before I actually met him). It didn't matter that we were strangers, that we might never meet; what mattered was a kind of loyalty and solidarity that are bred into you, and that can never be learned.

As for my own sense of Richards' artistic merits, I agree completely with Sheldon Currie and Alistair MacLeod that Richards will endure as one of the literary giants of the twentieth century. I've said as much elsewhere, and to the many hundreds of students I've had over the years, all of whom, it should be noted, were mesmerized by Richards' prose. Ranking artists, I know, is a mug's game, analogous to placing Bobby Orr over Wayne Gretzky, but I play the game because it has cultural currency. That Richards is without a doubt the most admired *and* berated *and* misunderstood Canadian writer of the century is a reflection, albeit refracted, of the power and precocity of his vision. In a culture in which literacy has become institutionalized and bound up in the ideologies of the academy, he makes professional readers uncomfortable, and accountable. Like many of the great writers before him, he gathers the truth claims of the social register and molds those into art so that we may see in his work a distillation of who we are as a people. In the process, he turns on their ears our much-vaunted principles (and proponents) of social justice, enlightened attitudes, and progressive ideologies. He is our great moralist, as Morley Callaghan was for too-brief a period, as Kafka and Melville were, both dying broke and unrecognized in their time.

The quality I admire most about Richards, then, is his bravery. For twenty-five years he has paddled a wide stretch of river against the wind and against the current, and he has done this mostly alone. He has battled poverty, alcoholism, scorn, and the intolerance of his own people (the worst of all possible ridicules) for the realization of his art. In his own essay in this collection he chastises himself for ruining most of his personal relationships, for flinching duties, and for failing in innumerable ways both himself and those around him. And all this, he admits, for the realization of his art, all for the preservation of the imaginative space necessary to remain true to his duty to his work. That is the price of art in the twentieth century! That is what's necessary, concurs Larry Mathews, in a culture of critics. I cannot imagine such perseverance or such guts. I cannot imagine such single-mindedness. But neither can I imagine a society worth living in without them.

I therefore agree with Currie and MacLeod that Richards is one of our literary giants, and I value their opinions because they too have created fine and lasting works of art. Ezra Pound used to ask critics, "what have *you* made?," a question with as much relevance today as when Pound uttered it. Well, in my own limited way, this collection of essays and anecdotes is what I, as a critic, can make. And, in making it, I have been guided by Anatole France's insistence that good criticism is the record of minds' journeys through great art. This collection, then, is the record of readers' journeys through Richards' fictional world. While many of the contributors will be familiar, they were not solicited or did not come forward on the basis of being expert witnesses but because they were readers themselves. Scholarship as philological indulgence does not exist in this collection. Scholarship as deep reading does. And at the end of the day the latter is the only kind of scholarship that matters.

As a long-time Richards reader myself, I was struck by the moments of recurrence in the pieces that follow, moments that confirmed many of my own intuitions about Richards and that have helped me find the language to write about those intuitions. I was struck first by the personal investment of all the contributors, especially by their willingness to write about their intensity of feeling, for to write passionately today about an artist is to risk being labelled a sycophant. The only conclusion that I can draw from this "willingness to risk" is one I have been struggling to articulate myself for some time now: that the honest reader simply cannot be indifferent to Richards' fiction. Richards himself has been instrumental in showing his readers the way here, specifically in showing his readers how to read, and many of the contributors below (and many before them) have picked up on this, describing his relationship with his characters as eerily realistic, if that is possible. Many marvel at his closeness to his characters; many recall incidents when he'd actually alter his own perspective to render theirs. So unique is his fiction that, like Flaubert and Joyce before him, he has had to teach us how to read. And, as Wayne Johnston and others have commented, to listen to Richards read and speak about his characters is to be ushered into his larger vision. His fiction, then, implicates his readers (as it implicates its author), and readers intelligent and sensitive and honest enough to understand this cannot be indifferent to it.

I was struck also by his readers' familiarity with his imagined world. Many of the contributors in this collection cite favourite characters and episodes toward what is a visceral understanding of fictional context. As a professor of literature, I can say with certainty that this is very rare, and very precious. Dickens had that effect on readers, and so did Twain, but few other writers since, and no other Canadian writer that I know of, with the possible exception of Stephen Leacock. I suspect Herb Wyile's inference is correct that this familiarity is related to Richards' seldom recognized role as a humorist (and, as such, a humanist). Readers relate to the comic, the absurd, and the unexpected; and they generally don't find these in today's serious fiction. So when Sadie's clan yells at the television because it says bad things about them, or when Nevin's first wife Gail (with cookie flour on her chin) restores to him the dignity he's lost, we nod silently with the truth, absurdity, and surprise of the situation. To appreciate Richards, then, is often to recollect the particular in celebration of the whole. His world is organic and infused with spirit; three-dimensional, it is a realm of ideas and personalities in action.

I observe also in the pieces that follow a tremendous range of response to Richards' work, everything from Frances MacDonald's contemplation of Richards' women to Bill Connor's thoughts on heroic action to Russell Perkin's exploration of Richards' (small "c") catholicism. I attribute this

range to the richness of Richards' work, to the mul-
tiple points of entry and exit he has created for
readers, even those his work challenges, the academics. Most revealing of all, perhaps, is *their*
response to him in this collection. While they
acknowledge his snubs, his academic readers are not
put off by them, more often than not agreeing with
the truth of his claims. As Fred Cogswell reminds
us, we academics are gadflies, though we hope not
to the degree of the Christopher Wheems.

I will observe finally what some have said
directly and what others have implied: in a word,
Richards' *humanity*. His kindness and generosity
are mentioned frequently in this collection, as is his
quick defense of the weak and the powerless. Many
write about the experience of meeting him as a
before-and-after experience. Many cite his humility
and his intolerance of pretense. What these obser-
vations have in common is a deep sense of pride
that Richards is one of us, that he is writing our
story. And notoriety, I suspect, has nothing to do
with this pride. Rather, his careful readers champion his vision. They know how rare it is that humanism and craft combine; and they know that the
result is great art.

From the beginning, I envisioned this collection,
which assembles many of the finest minds that have
written about Richards so far, as serving two pri-

mary purposes: first, as enriching an understanding of Richards' work, and, second, as being a starting point for scholarly investigation. Toward those ends, I have included a bibliography of Richards' creative works and a short bibliography of secondary sources by contributors. Because Richards is at the top of his form and because his readership is expanding rapidly, I expect that these bibliographies will soon have to be updated. But they are a place to start.

Lastly, I would be remiss if I did not acknowledge the following help: St. Thomas University, particularly Susan Parsons and Margie Reed, for research and editorial support; Ian Colford and Collette Saunders at *Pottersfield Portfolio* for their assistance with the original project; and, most importantly, Ellen Rose, for her substantial editorial help and encouragement. I would also like to acknowledge the tremendous good will of all the contributors assembled here, and would like to thank David Richards for allowing us to print his original essay.

Aside from buying books, readers have few other ways of showing appreciation for writers. I therefore dedicate this collection, on behalf of his readers, to David Richards, with our thanks and indebtedness.

May 1998/January 2002, Fredericton, N.B.

Remembering My Evaluators While Packing to Leave Home

DAVID ADAMS RICHARDS

(With thanks to Geoffrey Cook)

I have a picture of myself when I was Writer-in-Residence at the University of Ottawa in 1992. A woman telephoned one day and asked to do an interview with me. Her name sounded vaguely familiar.

"Oh yes," she said, surprised. "I didn't know you'd know of me. I wrote a review of your book *Nights Below Station Street*. I absolutely loved it."

I remembered her review, written four years previous to that phone call, written some months before *Nights* won the GG award – and I remembered she had on that occasion not loved it, dismissed it as a poor dour regionalist novel. I remembered where the review appeared, in the *London Free Press*.

The woman explained that she was now out of work, her unemployment was gone. She was trying to get hired by a certain FM radio station. For some reason she had told them she could get an interview with me. I didn't know how this would manage to get her anything, let alone a job, but thinking of the position she was in, of what it must have taken to phone me, I said of course.

She brought the tape recorder, did the interview, on a fall afternoon in my office at the University. I watched the tape recorder whirring about in front of her. I listened to her questions. A few days later she phoned, relieved to say that she had gotten the job, that the interview was exactly what *they* wanted. Thanked me. I said, "you're welcome." I never saw her again.

I usually do not refuse interviews because I put myself in the interviewer's shoes. Yet more and more I realize that interviewers don't ask me about my past, or who I am, so much as recount it to me.

Many times interviewers are fine and knowledgeable. And, more importantly, kind or kinder toward me than I was in granting to them the interview that they will be paid for. Yet on occasion, the other interviewer comes to visit. The interviewer who feels he/she knows me better than I am allowed to know myself. *Allowed* is the word.

And before they go, they ask for pictures. I have only a few. They are too important for me to give away. I find them, once again, when I am packing to leave for Toronto. They are memories of what the interviewers do not know.

They come out of the faded print of old

reviews, along with quotes from former acquaintances. Books written and inscribed to me by people I rarely see. Old pictures in rooms of former friends. Lobster parties down river of summers that are now gone.

I am somewhere in those pictures as well. Pictures of myself at twenty-one writing *The Coming of Winter* in an apartment in a house at 223 King Street in Fredericton with my cat Pushkin lying across my neck. The house was torn down years ago. The boys would drink beer and wine sitting on the steps outside. Sooner or later there'd be a fight. In the one apartment above us, two or three families lived, squabbled, and our mail was rifled through to see if we were getting money. Unfortunately for all concerned, we weren't.

Pushkin, a little grey female, disappeared one day, and my wife Peg went out to search for her, rain or shine. Finally she brought home this large grey tom, with its tail half chewed away, delighted that she had found our Pushkin again. The old tom must have been bemused, gobbling up his dinner, and wondering what he had done to deserve such sudden attention. We were twenty-one at the time, and hope was like that.

There is a picture of us taken six months before then – when we lived in a single room on Aberdeen Street in Fredericton. The bathroom was two flights up. We had a hot plate, a single cot, and I wrote at the table we ate on, late at night.

"I'm going to be a writer," I told Peg the first night I met her in November of 1967, at the skating rink (I couldn't skate, I never could, but I always went to the rink with friends). I think by the time we moved into that little room on Aberdeen she was realizing that I was damned to do it, and had doomed her. She had come from a family of nine children and a widowed mother, and married a man who had no money and no prospects of ever earning any. Expelled from high school three times, he was forced to see a psychiatrist before he was allowed to graduate. (The day I went to see the psychiatrist my poor worried mother bought me a new sports jacket and loafers – hoping to fool him.)

Later I managed to flunk all matrics except two, and the only way I got into university was by a kind of special dispensation, handed to me by St. Thomas. Not the saint. The university.

"Well, you did graduate?" the Registrar asked in embarrassment after looking over the blemishes on my record.

"Well – I think so, I'm almost sure I did – yes," I said, hopefully.

Hope. That was the thing. It carried us along as far as it could. I started my first novel in that small room on Aberdeen Street, called *The Keeping of Gusties*. It was never published, although an excerpt of it was.

I have a few pictures where I am sitting with

various other writers when I am about twenty-three. Some are famous, some are not.

In one, *The Coming of Winter* is being launched. I know because I am wearing my "about-to-be-published-for-the-first-time" suit jacket that Peg bought me for my birthday. And this picture is a reminder of that celebration. I should also remember always just how much of her week's wage that jacket cost her. The writers in this picture are all older than me by fifteen or twenty years, academic and tenured. Many had the prevalent modern flaw of mistaking being nice for being good, being compliant for taking a moral stand.

In another picture, I am with a group of young men and women at an English seminar in 1973, just before I quit university for good to finish writing *Blood Ties*.

Their faces come back and I remember the names. Unfortunately, I don't know where most of them are now. We were all considered the best of friends back then. For a few months I was as close to some in this group as I have ever been to any in my entire life.

Still, I don't believe I was in step with them, although in that seminar I made a concerted effort to be. I read the books, did the papers, was attentive. Thought of getting a degree, getting a doctorate, living a professorial life. But in the end I couldn't do it, and lost touch over the years with them all.

There were about eleven young men and

women in that seminar in 1973. But I don't remember where the picture was taken. One of the men came to a reading I did at Harbourfront in Toronto a few years ago. I phoned a woman in the group for the last time five or six years ago, one nostalgic winter night when I was down in Virginia. Another wrote me a letter which I procrastinated answering until I misplaced the address. Someone sent me a card after reading a story about me in *Maclean's* magazine.

I saw another after eighteen years when I was Writer-in-Residence in Vancouver. We literally bumped into each other in the lobby of the hotel I was staying at. She gave me her address, told me to phone. I said I would. But I never got to see her again. She was killed the next Christmas coming back home to the Miramichi. Meeting her that one last time seems more preordained than accidental because I had grown up with her, known her since I was four years old, and she was the very first person to be kind enough to read anything I had written. She was the person I trusted to write notes to the teachers when I was absent from high school for most of my last year there. This ruse went on, but finally we were both caught in the conspiracy, and I'm sorry I got her involved in it now. Her name was Karen.

I met one of the men from that seminar on a plane to Toronto one night when my wife, oldest son, and I were on our way to England. He asked me to write, gave me his address, asked me to send one of my books to his kids. I didn't get to it.

I think I know where the group picture of that seminar was taken but can't be sure. It was at one of the professor's houses – but I keep thinking of two houses at the same time and have probably gotten them confused.

That confusion reminds me of being in Australia with my family in 1993. Peg took a video of John Thomas and me walking across the bridge in Melbourne, near the art center where I was to read. The first few times he viewed the video, John Thomas remembered where we were and what we were talking about. And then he forgot what we were talking about. And recently when he saw it, he forgot where it was we were.

I stand in my study surrounded by books on shelves and books packed away, and papers boxed and ready to be sent to the archives in Fredericton.

My whole life has been parcelled out in books, and the writing of books. Half of my high school days were missed because I was up all night writing, and couldn't make it to class. Finally I was expelled in grade eleven and given the strap before I was allowed to go back the next year, by the same principal who recommended me for psychiatric treatment. I didn't care about being strapped, but I was in a funny position – to be beaten and forced to see a psychiatrist, so I would be allowed access to someplace I never really wanted to be.

I can't say if much was expected of me by those who evaluated me with psychiatric discussions and tests in the winter of 1968. They collected samples of my poetry to investigate. (The poetry wasn't very good.) Peg – who didn't need to – stood beside me throughout.

In order to fight back I became more determined in my resolve. School didn't interest me, and I didn't interest them, so I kept searching for places to write.

Writing (and how I thought about the world in order to write and what I wrote *about*) wasn't a decision I made for myself. I did not go to school and suddenly *find* writing. I did not join a writer's group or club, or think writing fanciful or outrageous. I thought writing was just the opposite of fanciful or outrageous.

From the time I was nineteen I was a writer and would have no *real* job, no academic position, no money except the little Peg or I earned, have no union, pay into no pension, receive no unemployment insurance, take no welfare, belong to no workgroup, have no political party I trusted. "I'm a writer," I said, like a broken record.

It is what I told the teacher who expelled me in grade eleven, and the psychiatrist too. It is what I told those who caught me in the town's library one winter afternoon, writing my first early story, "Old Man's Town." It is what I later told the professors. Or in fact what I *didn't* tell anyone ever. For I couldn't really speak of it. And I was never able to answer my evaluators very well at all back then. Even if my mom got me those new loafers, I don't think we fooled very many people.

All of that was so long ago now. And I have found that writers are forever on their own. And there is always manifest a realization, that it is still (and always will be) the evaluator's world. They hold the trump cards almost all the time.

Yet though it is the evaluator's world, people, wherever they may be from, or whatever they might do, are fearful of being evaluated, so they join together in political parties and groups, hold literary festivals, become members of writer's unions, teacher's unions, and editorial boards, or huddle the day away in taverns, so they will not feel the drafts of cold. And though I might have flinched in everything in my life, failed in everything, and ruined every personal relationship I might have had, I have not flinched in my duty to my work. The evaluators will have every other victory but not that. For I have written the books I have written.

I have found that no spirit can be crushed or humbled by someone's evaluation of spirit. And no disapproving high school teacher can crush you, and no failed grade, and no smirking jibe by a well-heeled tenured professor, when you yourself are making nothing – or no clandestine fax sent by the

publisher of a local paper who exalts in your casti-
gation, or no false friend, or self-seeking literary
gadfly sent out to interview you in the night, or no
disdain by former love, or no gutless tavern boy's
hard and disapproving glare. For I have faced all
that.

And there is another picture, one more.

In this picture I am thirty years old. I have
reached the age Peg once told me she was afraid I
would never reach. I am drinking with my boyhood
friends. I have swollen up to 189 pounds. Soon – in
another year or so – I will manage to quit drinking.

I look at this picture now, and I think back over
the years. I was thirty years of age then. I was writing *Lives of Short Duration*. Most of my university
friends had gone on to that professional world
where they earned thousands a year. The year
before I had earned $573.83.

But *Lives* got a bit of attention. And, through
many ups and downs in the last seventeen years,
and many harsh evaluations, so did certain subsequent novels, so that I now look upon my life as a
writer in two parts – before and after that novel.
And my past sometimes seems a vague and distant
past.

Yet still, and after all is said and done, I sometimes ache at night to revisit the people in those pictures, just once more. But they are all gone now,
and I can't get through to tell them anything. To tell
them that I have searched for them in the faces of

children, or in airport queues as far away as Melbourne, Valencia, and Madrid. That at times I thought I had come across them again, somewhere, in some airport lounge when I was travelling. Just once more.

And I would tell them, in the ways that have counted, that the evaluators did not win by my journey to the office of the psychiatrist when I was a kid of seventeen. And that I am grateful for whatever *true* friendship I have received from any Maritimer I have met. For the Maritimes *is* my country.

And I would add this about Maritimers: that I know as well as most, how they laughed, and danced in joy, and were brave, and bright, and proud, and kind, and heroic, and loved their kin and land as much as I, and smiled when their heart was broken.

But I know this too, I know it all too well: no matter how long I stare at the pictures, reach out to those gone, make fumbling attempts to touch the youthful faces of those I once loved, it won't help. It doesn't help at all anymore. For the ghost I am staring at is me.

An Interview with David Adams Richards

TONY TREMBLAY

TT: In as much as you can talk about it – some novelists don't like to – what are you currently
working on?

DAR: Well neither do I, but, in brief, I'm working
on a novel that I hope will be finished this summer [2002]. It is based in part on the life of my
grandmother, who opened up a theatre business
here on the river in 1911-12 era, and the theatre lasted until the 1980s. It revolves around
her career and her life, and the lives of my family, fictionally, of course.

TT: What compelled you to write about your
grandmother's story?

DAR: Because I've always thought that women
were great human beings. And they didn't
become great because the1960s happened;
they were great human beings before that. One
of these great women was my grandmother –
both my grandmothers, in fact. But Janie, who
I'm writing about, was a fabulous woman,
gutsy as hell. She had her own business in an
age when it wasn't really known for women to

have businesses. So her story is very compelling.

TT: What was in her background that would have moved her to do something as daring and self-reliant as setting up a business in the very new medium of film?

DAR: From all reports she was an absolute virtuoso on the violin, which she called a fiddle. She was drawn to the stage because of her own performing and because of the vaudeville era she lived through. She married a traveling musician from England, and they set up the business together. My uncles and cousins are fine painters, as was my father, a fine painter and musician. So there was that world of art in my background. That being as it may – and I don't want to be implicated in a family history of artists – my art is very different than the kind of art my grandmother would have approved of. Her art was more of a public, performance-based art. The subtle overlay of personal politics in my own work would have been hard for her to examine, nor should she have to. I'm just saying that it is a very different world now.

TT: About those politics, I want to ask what has become the inevitable "regionalism" question. I think of William Carlos Williams' line about localism alone leading to culture. I consider your work very regional, and I consider that a great strength, but you've decried the regional label. Why?

DAR: Well no, not really. I've decried how it's used by people who can't see past their noses. I haven't decried that I write from a particular region. I think the word is not intended to mean localism and fidelity in the way certain – that is, most – literary critics use it. They use the word to imply that regional work is not worthy of their examination. That it doesn't deal with humanity in the way they define humanity, which I think is utter nonsense. What is at fault is their usage of the word. It's not that I don't write from a particular region. Of course I do.

TT: It has taken you a long time, fifteen books, to construct and populate that very unique region in your work that may or may not be "Miramichi." Certainly your novels are set there, but your work, in a larger sense, also establishes a place of its own. Your writing is rare in Canadian and western literature in that regard. Your writing may have grown from a real place, but it is also a territory onto itself. Do you agree with this?

DAR: Yes, I'm doing things that are created in my own fictional world that reflect a personal struggle toward defining my own vision of humanity. I don't think other writers from here or anywhere are doing what I am, or need to, for that matter. But I do. So it's a very personal kind of regionalism, if you want to call it that. And it can be a very scary place, partly because not too many people know what it is about. People who come to it cold often have no idea what it is about. At times, certain editors are appalled that I would say and write the things that I do. Sometimes the light comes on in their eyes, and other times I hit brick walls because people don't understand what I'm doing. But, you know, that's fine by me because, as you say, this is my own world.

TT: What does that mean, saying it is scary? That it torments you? Frightens you?

DAR: It doesn't torment or frighten me. But it frightens some people because, well, a lot of the things that are taken for granted in today's world about how people are and what they should be are challenged in my work, and a lot of times that bothers people.

TT: You are now with your third publisher. I want to ask you about your experience of the politics of Canadian publishing. What has your experience been in that world?

DAR: My third and probably my best publisher to date. At the beginning, when I was a kid, I dealt mainly with older people who told me what was good for my work. And a lot of times what they said was good for my work was really good for them. My first publisher, Oberon, received *The Coming of Winter* from a UNB professor who sent it with an attached letter – God only knows what was in that letter, but I had enough dealings with Oberon to know that it was about me being a sound writer from the Outback somewhere. Whether that was good or bad I paid my dues through that small publisher. Then I went to McClelland and Stewart, and it was fine for a while. I had a good editor there (and a good editor at Oberon, too, for that matter). I've had five editors now and any one of them could have edited any one of my books. None of them, however, could have written my books. That is the catch.

There is a certain attitude that editors develop toward your work that you sometimes agree with and sometimes don't. Doubleday didn't look at me at all as a regionalist or as a person from New Brunswick, but as one of the important writers in the country, and it's obvious they believe that. That attitude has opened a new audience for me. It is like looking at Alden Nowlan and saying that he's a regional poet, when in fact he towers over almost all other poets of the century in Canada.

TT: I want to push that just a little further. Stephen Henighan has a new book out about, in part, the centralist bias of Canadian publishing, particularly the Torontocentric vision of the country. I'm interested in the implications of that Torontocentric or centralist cultural mentality because it strikes me that what a publisher from there wants from a writer who comes from the regions is more regionalism, more of what they would define as exotica – lighthouses and fishing boats from the east coast, for example.

DAR: Of course they do, that's why if you write intelligently from the regions you risk being scorned. They can't find a place to put you, and they desperately need a place. But you have to remember this: most publishers don't have a clue what they want. They want last year's book, last year's big seller. Sometimes they pay wildly exorbitant up-front fees for a book that doesn't go anywhere, and pay next to nothing for a book that sells 200,000 copies. Even the regional publishers go to the centre in order to get their books circulating in Toronto or Montreal or Vancouver. So there is a self-defeatism even in the regions. But the thing to remember is that the urbancentric ideal is actually nebulous because centralist publishers themselves don't know what it is. They only assume they do, and, if you examine the record of their hits and misses, they are as fallible as anyone else.

TT: Why, then, did you move to Toronto?

DAR: Let's just say it had almost nothing to do with Toronto and everything to do with New Brunswick.

TT: I imagine, like most artists, you think of your

career as having distinct phases. How does your current work differ from your early work?

DAR: In some ways it doesn't. I'm interested in the same thing – that minute interchange between human beings on a certain level that causes all the grandeur and all the heartbreak. In that sense my work is unchanged. But I am far more faith-based now than I was. I believe that there is a definite structure within the human consciousness and spirit that can help us overcome almost any difficulty. And that's the real resource of mankind. There is an interior world and an exterior world, and we all live in the interior world, the one we don't show. That's the real world. Now, this isn't new, and it isn't new to me, and it isn't even new to my work because I was saying this as far back as *The Coming of Winter*, but I just wasn't saying it the way I'm saying it now. With *The Bay of Love and Sorrows* and *Mercy Among the Children* and this present book I am examining that inner world more deeply and in greater detail.

TT: Did you have to mature into the ability to write about and explore that interior faith?

DAR: Probably. I had to go through certain things in my life. As a writer I had to be almost completely shunned, at times, by the outside world to realize that it was the inside world that mattered. So having experienced that when I was in

my thirties – having people, life-long friends,
turn their backs on me because my work wasn't
what they thought it should be – I began to realize that the inner world mattered far more than
the outer.

TT: Okay, but you are consciously exploring different types and layers of morality in your latest
novels, generally Christian and more specifically Catholic nuances. Do those formal religious
programmes play a part in your intentions as a
writer?

DAR: Catholicism plays a very big part, but I'm
almost always angst-ridden over the church and
have almost always embraced the faith. Even
when I was a kid, irreverence toward any faith
bothered me because I thought it was shallow.
Irreverence toward the organization, however,
could often make me laugh hilariously. The
organizations themselves not only were full of
bombast but at times were irreverent to the
faith. So you see it was the faith of Elly in *Mercy*
that I could cry over, but the faith of the priest,
Father Poirier, the embodiment of the church
hierarchy, is something that I've always ques-
tioned. And what does the church tend to do? It
tends to dismiss people like Elly.

I don't want to give the impression that the
difference is black and white because it is not.
However, faith will create a Saint Bernadette
and the church will create the Catholic

Women's League and the College of Cardinals. There is a big difference between those, between the saints and the bureaucrats. Conrad said that religion is for women and God is for men. In some ways that's completely wrong, but in another way absolutely true, because what Conrad meant is that organizational structures are domestic, whereas striving for faith and even martyrdom, regardless of gender, are militaristic activities, I mean internally. So we are dealing with a very strange duality here. On the one hand a blood in faith, and on the other a kind of domestic sanctuary. It is the blood in faith that I want to explore in my work. The criminality of the church is tragic, but the faith will continue to exist. There is no Cardinal that can usurp the faith, and no buggering priest can do it either.

TT: The most catholic of genres, I suppose, is the novel. Why is the novel *your* preferred form?

DAR: Because it is the only place I can hide all my mistakes, for one thing. Also, the epic structure of humanity has always interested me – the so-called "big picture of things" – and the novel seems to be fitted for that. I can simply do more in the novel form.

TT: How do you write a novel; what's your process?

DAR: I start with a character and a certain idea. In *For Those Who Hunt the Wounded Down*, for example, how does a man, Jerry Bines, who has done something terrible, try to atone for his life? Or Ruby taking Cindi under her wing in *Evening Snow Will Bring Such Peace*. For what purpose does Ruby do that when Ivan Basterache is Cindi's husband? That's what I wanted to explore. But you must understand that the process is quite nebulous – it starts with a feeling for the character, nothing mapped out. I think about how characters feel toward one another and what they are really saying between the lines. What is Ruby really doing? Well, Ruby is entertaining herself at Cindi and Ivan's expense. That's what critics miss.

You see, the problem of so much of the criticism in this country is that it harkens back to a Mother Goose story. Critics don't understand that people are flesh and blood, and that you can love them even though they create misery for themselves and others. Critics assume that I am moralizing against Ruby when I am doing nothing of the sort. I am saying that her action causes a tragedy, but I am not saying she is a bad person. I love Ruby, some aspects of her I love fiercely. The finest thing that was ever said of one of my characters was said by a Cree man. I was very down about the critical reception of *Evening Snow* at the time, and this man came up to me after a reading and said he had never read a character that represented the kids he'd grown up with on the reserve as well as Ivan Basterache. It was one of the nicest compliments ever given to me: it revealed his generosity, and showed that humanity is universal. So I was very happy to create Ivan for him.

TT: Have you made changes to your use of the novel as genre over your career?

DAR: Yes, *The Coming of Winter* is a very objective look at kids growing up. Then there was what I consider a breaking off point. In *Blood Ties*, where I was probably influenced by Faulkner and others, I became very subjective. And I had difficulty breaking out of that subjectivity. It took *Lives of Short Duration* and *Road to the Stilt House* to get away from that subjectivity and get back to an analytical survey of humanity, which I prefer and have become very comfortable with. One of my editors a few years back said "you explain everything; you tell everything about everyone." I responded that it is only going to get worse because that is the course I am on in my literary life. I'm dealing with mankind in a way I know, and I'm going to tell what I know.

TT: You would agree, though, with the statement that your novels are more character driven than plot driven?

DAR: Almost always, although I am more interested in plot now, and have been for the last couple of novels. Plot itself, though, has never driven my work; the characters have. People say that my characters are alive to me, and that's true to a certain extent. They don't sit beside me or anything like that, but I defend them as if they are real, especially against shallow assumptions. The shallow assumption that Cecil is bad and Leah is good in *Blood Ties* that certain wives of university professors have always declared is one that I will defend against vigorously, for I love Leah and Cecil both. Cecil is the one who shows us how to love Leah, so how can you not love Cecil? If you can't see that you've probably studied too much postmodernism.

TT: How long do you live with a character before you can write that character?

DAR: I'm not sure because before I sit down to write I don't know what characters I'll be writing about. Alistair MacLeod's stories are planned meticulously, and I admire that tremendously, but it is not how I work. I knew, for instance, that there would be a Janie in my current novel because she is the main character for the first part of the book, and I knew Miles, her son, would dominate the second part. But I didn't know that Rebecca, the nanny, was going to be the undercurrent of the book. There was a tragic link in their lives, but I didn't know she would be that link until I started writing.

TT: Your mention of postmodernism earlier leads

me to ask if literary theory can play a role in assessing your work?

DAR: It certainly plays a role in other people's assessment of my work. And this goes to a larger issue, which is that many professors of literature don't seem to have a clue about what they are reading. I really feel that. The Cree man I mentioned before is a good example of what I'm taking about. That this man from a reserve in northern Quebec understood Ivan Basterache more deeply and humanely than someone from the University of Toronto confirms my point. As I've said in the talks I've given, I feel that many literary critics in this country are intellectual illiterates; they have no idea what it is they are reading. Yet, ironically, their work forms the framework of what is thought to be the most informed and enlightened criticism of our time. For some writers, this intellectual illiteracy is terribly unfortunate; for others, it is very opportune. I seem to be in the first group.

TT: Has criticism ever helped your own work?

DAR: Probably, but I wouldn't be able to say how specifically. Writers listen to their critics, even if they say they don't. I'm sure, then, that criticism has played some part in what I do.

TT: How would you like your work to be read?

DAR: I can't give an answer that isn't glib here. I would like it to be read from the beginning to the end. And read well – that is, thoughtfully and thoroughly.

TT: What has given rise to the anti-academic thread that has appeared in your work since *Hope in the Desperate Hour*?

DAR: I don't know how "anti" it is. I have tremendous compassion for Christopher Wheem in *Hope*. Certainly I have far more compassion for him than he has for the person he is going to visit, Vicki Shackle. But having said that I think his lack of self-understanding, his inability to know his own motives, is representative of the sadness of academia. Christopher Wheem is destroyed by himself in this book. He doesn't realize that the most important human trait is compassion – the very thing the academic world professes to teach, and, ironically, the very thing that his retarded son and near-illiterate wife have in abundance. The fact that the academic doesn't know this while the son and wife do compels me to examine that academic world. So that's what I did in *Hope*.

The academic community is a cloistered community, one that laughs and rails at all other cloistered communities. They rail against the Jesuits and the nuns, saying how terribly repressed these people are, when, in fact, the academic community is one of the most cloistered of all. It believes in the answers that it has created for itself. And that has to be examined.

Many of these people, the Christopher Wheems, started out in grade one and have never left school. And that has to be examined. Some of them became furious with me because they heard that my grandmother had money, which, in their mind, should have forbidden me from writing about Kevin Dulse [*The Coming of Winter*]. Well, not only did I live like Kevin Dulse most of my life, but I knew and grew up with a hundred Kevins. The academics assumed that money forbids you to know these people because they have refused in their own minds to know these people. And that also has to be examined. And so I have examined it, and I have paid the price for that examination.

The outrage over my novels comes mostly from these types – academics or intellectuals who work for the CBC. Their criticism of my work can be self-serving and hypocritical because it says that Dave Richards is not allowed to say this and that about us, but we can say anything about his characters and him. My grandmother, you know, hated education. And why shouldn't she; she had grade eight and was bullied constantly by people at the bank with more education than she had. She tried to get across the river in the middle of the night at one point to get money to save her business, and there were men there to try to stop her – some of them, educated men. There are many things about my grandmother that I could question, but her dislike of that kind of education isn't one of them. I've always resented the idea that books could teach us how to treat people. The only thing that can teach us how to treat others is our own humanity, which we don't have to learn from a book.

TT: How accommodating is Canada to artists?

DAR: Canada is very accommodating to the poster boys and girls of the artistic elite, but it is not very accommodating to those who refuse to be pin-ups. Simply put, you have to fit into one of the requisite slots. You have to be good copy. If you fit into one of the slots – regionalist, environmentalist, social activist – then you are wonderful. If not, you are on your own. But the CBC, the most outrageously politically correct organization in the western world, only pretends to know its country; in fact, it dictates to the country what it feels the country should know. If you happen to find that false, as some do, then you are going to be heckled or shunned, neither of which is helpful for the artist. What is really unfortunate about this is that so many don't find fault with it. I believe that those kinds of experiences allow artists to pay their dues. And all true artists pay their dues in one way or another. The trick, sometimes the miracle, is to survive intact.

TT: Travel has been important for you. You travel a

lot, and you like to be on the move. What is travel about for you?

DAR: Keeping away from myself, I suppose. Trying to run away. The problem with travel, as someone once said very well, is that you have to bring yourself along. We all have our own ghosts and demons, and that's part of why I am always on the move. I wrote a poem once in an airport very far from home. I had my son, John Thomas, in my arms, he was about four at the time, and the poem was about my experience of thinking that maybe here, at last, is where it would all be better. It wasn't, of course, but every new place offers the possibility that it might.

TT: You've said that writers often have an instinct for life that can never be taught, even by life experience. What do you mean by this? And where does that instinct for life come from? Are you born with it?

DAR: Well, perhaps, but I'm not sure. I know of people from my early days at McCord Hall who were much older but could never have written *The Keeping of Gusties*, my first [unpublished] novel, completed when I was twenty-one. Most of what I think of as "instinct" comes from self-examination, especially when one is a teenager. It is the self-examination that allows you to know other people. It is not the examination of other people that allows you to know them –

that is reporting, not insight. Only from self-examination can come *War and Peace*.

Where does it come from? It probably is rooted, first, in seeing things differently, and then in examining and coming to grips with why you see things differently. This happens at an early age, and doesn't much change for writers. It's not because writers are enclosed, but because we have formed, through self-examination, a vision of the world that we are trying to explore. To give that vision up is to give that exploration up. So why would we change it?

TT: Well, I have to ask, then, what it is in a kid that allows or forms that aptitude for self-examination? There must be something there. What is it?

DAR: I can only answer that question by way of my own work. Orville and Rance are on the beach in *Blood Ties*. And all of a sudden Orville says he knows why the ice is like it is, and why the shoreline is like it is, and why the birds are like they are, and Rance doesn't. You see, the catch, or what that whole idea turns on, is that Rance doesn't know. And what is surprising is not that Orville knows but that Rance, who should know, doesn't. When you see, as a kid, that the world doesn't really know some of the things you believe the world knows, that makes a strong impression. That revelation moved me to write about what they, the Rances of the

world, should know, and about why the
Orvilles of the world do know.

TT: If you hadn't been a writer, what would you
have been?

DAR: A doctor. I wish I could alleviate suffering
more. Doctors can't always alleviate suffering,
but at least they can put their feet in and help.

TT: After all this time – thirty years and close to
twenty books – how do you look back on your
career?

DAR: I did what I had to do.

A Lad Around Town

WAYNE CURTIS

I ran a store in Newcastle for twenty-odd years commencing in the late 1960s. During this time I did business with everyone in town and indeed the Miramichi region. I had been born on the river and was deep-rooted and comfortable there. Like many of the river's young, I had been to Ontario and had returned. While I came from farther up river, ours is small enough an area that everybody eventually gets to know everybody else, their genealogy and philosophy. This, plus doing business there, gave me a certain "pulse" of the town. I was never proud of the fact that I was a store keeper, and I mention it now only as a qualifier. Truth is, I had come home to write.

But the store front on the square in Newcastle gave me one advantage. I was able to watch many of the town's young grow, educate themselves, and move into the world. One of the youths to press his face against my store windows was David Adams Richards. He was just another young lad about town, sandy haired and muscular, who walked with a bit of a limp. He appeared rough at the edges and I found out early enough that he would fight if someone he cared about or someone who was physically handicapped was being mistreated. (His friends had nick-named him "Rocky.") David was a good scrapper for his size, and for this I envied him.

But David Adams Richards was not just another tough youngster who hung out at the hockey rinks or scrapped in the streets. This kid was an avid reader with somewhat of a cultured interior, having come from a more artistic background than the others. Not that this drew him apart from them; it was just something I observed. His grandparents had been classical musicians who ran the river's Opera House in the old days and his father ran a theatre up on Pleasant Street and the Mid-Way drive-in over in Bushville.

The Richards lived in the part of Newcastle known to us as "The Rocks." David and his friends grew up skating down by Ritchie's Wharf, running the roofs of empty box-cars sitting on the siding, smoking in alleys, and shouting at the young girls who walked with their mothers about town. Later they would sit and drink beer or rum over at the Legion on Hanover Hill or at the Dalton's Black Horse Tavern down on Castle Street. (Here a cop once fired a shot into the air to break up a fist-fight and narrowly missed a man sleeping in the stairs over the bar.) But mostly David and his friends hung out on the river. They would balance themselves high above the town on the steel spans of the old Morrisey Bridge with its rumble of trucks below and dive into thirty metres of murky water. At the

waterfront when cargo ships came in from foreign
lands, it was said they purchased vodka, using the
coupon-money they had gathered from the
Canadian Tire store in Chatham. They were, let me
say, adventuresome.

At St. Mary's Roman Catholic church on the
hill, the Rev. Henry McGrath made futile attempts
each Sunday to set the boys straight. Among the
youths in the pew with David would be his friends
Peter Baker, Giles Kenny, Peter McGrath, Trapper
Newman, Richard Parker, and Bruce Wallace.
Though I knew them all, I never broke into their
circle because I was older and, of course, I had
come from out of town.

Newcastle was a false-fronted clapboard town
then, rugged in ways yet sophisticated in others.
Much like David himself. In the 1970s Newcastle
started to change when the big malls came. And like
its giant elm trees that once shaded the square, the
wooden buildings started to decay and were being
hacked away. So went the diners like the Shamrock
on Pleasant, Dick's Lunch on Jane, and Susie
O'Brien's on Henry Street. So went the old inns like
The Ideal, The Elm, and the Royal Hotel with their
rocking-chaired verandas and resident old men who
cooked on hot-plates in the stairs. The Victorian
town had become a scattered array of brick malls
and concrete bridges which eventually amalgamated
with Chatham and the surrounding villages to
become the City of Miramichi.

David grieves the loss of this place of inno-
cence, and though time has already made Newcastle
indistinct, the old town (as we knew it) continues to
live strongly in his prose. In that prose we can see
the old hotels, the taverns, rinks, churches, schools,
and the old movie house. The sulphur smells from
the mill, the pockets of laughter from the wharf, the
brown moving river, and across it, the slanting and
twisted shacks of Chatham Head, a place we
referred to then as Verdun. This world is preserved
in Richards' novels. His sentences are short and
blunt, yet descriptive with always an element of fear
– the fear of feuding communities, tough cops, and
abundant criminals.

When David's first book, *The Coming Of
Winter*, was published by Oberon in 1974, I immediately ran out and purchased a copy. When I started to read, I wished I had written it. In his first
attempt, David had captured the town's youths and
their causes. And David was still so young. By the
time his great book, *Nights Below Station Street*,
won the Governor General's award in 1988, I was
getting to know Dave better. We had golfed together, I had kept up with his many books and films, and
I was impressed with how he was handling his success. He was still one of us – down-to-earth, but his
own man. He had become a writer's writer.

By the late 1980s, I had built a cabin in the
Upper Blackville area on the Main Southwest
Miramichi. I had given up the store and was sum-

mering there, working as a river guide. Dave was Writer-in-Residence at the University of New Brunswick and was coming to fish off and on, a thing that has since grown into a tradition of sorts, regardless of where he lives. We cook and talk into the nights, and we cover a lot of territory. We talk about our boxing hero Roberto Duran (nicknamed "fists of stone"), the rugged World Middleweight Champion from Panama, and talk about Dickens, Keats, Tolstoy, good hockey, and fly-fishing. We talk about writing and the politics in the arts that we both despise. He sleeps in my son's old bedroom under a too-small sleeping bag. He knows that room is open to him and sometimes he comes and stays without as much as calling. On the river he helps me to celebrate successes I may have had in writing. He has never missed one of my launches. But more importantly he is always willing to listen to the heartaches I have suffered while struggling to accomplish what I have.

"What time should we get up in the morning?" he asks, one night before taking his son John off to bed.

"I think nine would be time enough," I say. "If we're on the river by ten o'clock we will be okay." I tell him this because most of the fish we have caught have been at approximately eleven am or seven pm. And I have been on the river forty-eight days this summer.

"Good enough," he says and the lights go out.

In the morning for some reason I am up early and preparing breakfast. I decide to call him at eight.

"What time is it?" comes an irritated groggy voice from his room.

"Eight!"

"But I thought we were getting up at nine?" he growls.

"Well . . . I was *up* and . . . well, there's no foam on the water . . . and it's going to rain later on . . . and it's . . . I think we should go sooner that's all . . . this time anyway."

"Well, whatever ya think then."

After breakfast, the three of us drive in my old pick-up truck, young John Thomas sitting between David and me, asking a hundred questions about fish and birds and even books. At a pool called Mercury Island, I take John Thomas' picture sitting on the tailgate in his old straw hat, looking like a Mark Twain character. Then David and I start to fish seriously while John wades in the shallows where he skips rocks and tries to build a sand castle out of blue stones. Around eleven, Dave, who is ahead of me in the pool, hooks into a salmon. It is a big fish with a lot of fight and the water is fast and in the salmon's favour. When it is finally landed we instruct John Thomas to take our picture, and we stand together with the fish. This shot is for David's new fishing book.

Later we leave our waders and fly-vests on and

drive to another pool. Along the way we stop for something to eat and wear our fishing things into the restaurant. People stare, but this is the country's best known salmon river, and we are just hanging out and enjoying the day. John Thomas tries to feed quarters into an ancient jukebox which doesn't work. David talks like he writes: blunt and sharp yet descriptive. "Who gives a piss. I mean, we're not changing just to come in here and eat," he says grinning. And I see again he is still a man of no pretense.

Hunting Richards'
Novels Down

MARGO WHEATON

In the mid-1980s, as part of my English degree
requirements, I wrote a thesis about the first four
novels by David Adams Richards, an author introduced to me by my father who, in the same rever-
ential tone he usually reserved for talk about the
Miramichi River, handed me a copy of *Lives of
Short Duration* and said "Read *this*." Writing that
thesis was utter hell, not just because of the usual
demands of such projects, but due to a strange
sense of guilt that plagued me throughout the
entire exercise, an unshakable feeling of wrongdoing that was as keen and immediate as the novels'
poetic and powerful scenes. Though I could not
articulate nor understand it, I was seized by the
distinct feeling that, in analyzing them, I was committing a fundamental wrong against these books I
so deeply loved, that in some inexplicable way, I
was committing an act of violence. I dutifully
slaved through the assignment, the feeling of
wrongdoing growing blacker and heavier with
each sentence. I constructed a theoretical framework, thesis sentence and conclusion, relinquished

all 110 pages to my advisor, and carried my confusion instead.

Years later, in 1995, I stumbled upon an essay in
Brick Magazine written by Tony Tremblay in which,
after describing his years-long fascination with
Richards' work, he confessed his current inability to
begin an article that would "contain the elusive
essence or subtext of his art" and declared that he
had "come to realize . . . that scholarly frameworks
and academic tropes can never capture the life of
his work." I resonated with his mixed sense of wonder and perplexity; it brought back the old sense of
guilt and betrayal. But of what?

Or whom. Reading through the reviews and
critical articles I had collected over the years, I was
again face to face with interpretations I had turned
to years ago for help in writing about Richards'
characters. Over and over, characters who I loved
and identified with were described as "uncivilized,"
"violent," "repulsive," and even, according to one
article, downright "evil." As the dates of the reviews
and articles moved closer to the present, the blatant
appearance of such negative one-word labels started to lessen but I was still struck by the sheer per-
sistence of descriptions of his characters based primarily in terms of social station and circumstance.
Many of the reviews I read were not, as before,
decrying or simply wondering at Richards' supposed attachment to lower-class society but seemed,
now, to be unconsciously invoking a concept of

Richards as a spiritual spokesperson for the region. The wide-spread appearance of meaningful religious terms like "sin," "redeem," "crucified," and "bearing witness" in articles that were still describing Richards' characters with words like "violent," "irrational," "working-class," "desperate," and "semi-literate" seemed dangerously close to a kind of literary charity. It was as if Richards, besides being cast in the role of regional representative for the marginalized and presumably inarticulate was responsible for redeeming them too. As though it was the force and existence of the author's sympathy, more so than the dignified personal qualities his characters revealed, that could convince readers that Richards' characters had souls worth cherishing.

While deep concern and empathy is certainly part of Richards' attachment to his characters, describing his intricate and intense relationship with them as fundamentally grounded in sympathy says too much about their frailties and sufferings and too little about the author's fierce affection for them, of his sheer delight in their vitality, humour, strength, generosity, and courage. As I had painfully discovered writing my thesis, highlighting single aspects of Richards' work leaves out so much.

As in the Dostoevsky novels that he admires, Richards' characters are relentlessly complex; part of both novelists' tasks is to witness the depths of vast and complicated souls in all their dimensions. When I first read the fluid, searching prose of the early novels, I was amazed at how naturally the characters seemed to be unfolding, not only to me as a reader but to the narrator as well as he faithfully followed them, discovering their rich inner worlds. Such writing has less to do with the charitable act of compassion and more to do with a visionary seeing and thinking that is the product of an uncompromising and active love. Richards has said in interviews that he writes from and of the heart; perhaps that is why he continually sees in his characters what is essential, sees them outside of fixed, rigidly-defined frameworks of social and narrative thought. It is only by rejecting sweeping assumptions and the safety of labels that a character like Cecil in *Blood Ties*, for example, can be believably cast as a man who is capable both of hurling his young son against a stove in a fit of anger and of carrying a dead infant protectively in his hands, bare-chested in a snowstorm.

The emotional range and honesty of these early novels riveted me; here were human beings in all their immense, contradictory shades of light and darkness. Here were novels that had as their foundation the matter-of-fact acceptance of the limitations of living, of drunkenness, poverty, despair, isolation, and self-interest. And yet, even with a full presentation of these stifling conditions, here also were novels with an aching sense of the inherent beauty, transcendence, and mystery of the human heart.

Reading these novels, I did encounter a marked sense of the characters' "otherness," but not the kind so often found in writing on Richards' work. These novels were asking me, as a reader, to consider and honour characters who would consistently transcend description, assumptions, and categorization.

Richards is still, a decade later, inviting me to think in radical terms, to approach his novels in a way that moves beyond categorical, prescriptive thinking; how else could you explain a magnificent character like Jerry Bines, the dark presence in *Road to the Stilt House* who becomes the self-sacrificing yet all-too-human ex-con protagonist of *For Those Who Hunt the Wounded Down*? And the choice is still there, always mine. I can respond to Jerry, and to any of Richards' characters, as Vera, the ambitious social worker, does, her theoretical structure and personal agenda intact as she sifts through his experience to strengthen her thesis about the meaning of his life as she constructs it, suppressing or simply failing to see aspects of his character and circumstance that don't fit into her narrowly-imagined framework.

Vera reflects Richards' radical conception of violence, one that exists as a possibility in every moment both inside and outside the world of the novel: to boil others down, not with fists but with thoughts and words, denying them their fundamental dignity. Though not entirely conscious or even intentional (Richards has Vera, at one moment in the novel, whispering "I'm sorry" as she intuits but does not comprehend the nature of her actions), the ultimate goal of all violence is effected: Jerry is diminished, reduced. For a writer like Richards who strives to view his characters in their totality this is more than tragedy.

There is a fundamental impulse inherent in literary criticism, as in other forms of critical thinking, that is intrinsically violent. Many of its tools are fashioned to break things apart, to classify, name, and define, to penetrate, seize, and to fix in order to get at the heart of a novel. To break into pieces in order to understand the whole. But Richards' uncompromising stance is the absolute irreducibility of the human personality, of the immense vastness of the human soul and a celebration of the mysteries Reason has ever been unable to fathom – like hope, self-sacrifice, beauty, and despair. Salvation and redemption. Compassion.

I have stopped trying to hunt the novels of David Adams Richards down. In the past decade, I have read them for their poetic beauty and vision, for their portraits of vibrant and astonishing characters, and to stand, with him, in a state of wonder at the improbable blessing of being alive. I have read Richards' novels, again and again, to learn how to love.

Small Heroics

WILLIAM CONNOR

Before going on to establish his reputation as a novelist, David Richards wrote poetry, a form that
allowed him to express his central creative concerns
more directly than fiction. His first published book
was a small collection of poems which appeared in
the New Brunswick Chapbook series in 1972. The
title, *Small Heroics*, echoed that of the collection's
shortest poem. "Small Heroics" is only three lines
long:

> They fan small wings to stay alive
> Yet fire rages round their hive
>
> In unison the choked bees die.

Although the poem is pared to essentials and does
not explain the source of the fire, it almost certainly refers to the traditional method in rural areas for
getting rid of unwanted bees' nests: wait till all the
bees come home in the evening and then set fire to
the nest. In the dark, the defending bees attack the
flames rather than the arsonist.

This is a deftly executed little poem in its own
right, capturing a small, self-contained community
being destroyed by external forces that its members

can neither appreciate nor, in spite of their unified heroics, successfully defend against. However, my main interest here is the striking appropriateness of this representation of insect lives of short duration as an introduction to Richards' fiction to come. The traditional culture and values of small communities are always under threat in Richards' novels, and, while probably not intended at the time, his representation of the beleaguered bees in "Small Heroics" certainly points toward the circumstances faced by his later fictional characters. Generally, Richards focuses on characters who are not attuned to the imported social and cultural trends, which, just as inevitably as the fire of the poem, are consuming their established ways of life. And, like bees in the night, these characters tend all too often to attack the flames while failing to identify their source.

As in "Small Heroics," fire is arguably the most important symbolic image in Richards' novels. The fire that marks characters like John Delano, Cecil, and George Terri in Richards' first trilogy symbolizes, among other things, their turbulent emotions and self-destructiveness. Many other characters suffer burns, and some, like Ivan Basterache in *Evening Snow Will Bring Such Peace*, and Garth and Penny Shackle in *Hope in the Desperate Hour*, die by fire. But fire in Richards' fiction is not simply destructive. It also holds the potential for purgation and renewal. In *For Those Who Hunt the Wounded*

Down, Jerry Bines is injured while burning his camp so that Gary Percy Rils will not be able to use it as a base of operations from which to exact his revenge on the community. Jerry's injuries represent his willingness to sacrifice himself if necessary, both in atonement for the mistakes of his earlier life and out of his unlearned sense of responsibility for people in his hometown. Arnold in *Road to the Stilt House* burns his dead brother's blood-stained clothing and then, in a final act of defiance against a life in which the cards have been so thoroughly stacked against him that even his family and his home can be taken away with impunity, he burns the stilt house itself. This act is partly rebellion and revenge, but it is also, and much more so, a symbolic purging of evil. In the memorable story "Kopochus 1825" and in the collective memory of Richards' fictional world, the great Miramichi forest fire that shaped the region in its infancy recurs as a symbol of renewal as well as destruction. While the death of the bees by fire in "Small Heroics" may be futile in the immediate context, the bees' characteristic readiness to defend their hive regardless of individual costs discourages casual attacks and in the long run helps to ensure the survival of the species. From first to last in Richards' published work, fire is a source of testing, and passing the test – as in the case of Ivan when he finds himself unable to abandon a horse in a forest fire – does not always entail individual survival.

"Small Heroics," then, introduces the concern with heroic action that remains central throughout Richards' novels. Heroics are hardly rare in fiction, of course, but in Richards' fiction heroics are of a special kind – "small" heroics, heroic actions that take place in limited circumstances, that are quite often futile, and that very frequently go unrecognized by those whose interests they serve. The essential features remain consistent throughout. Heroic actions are characterized by unselfishness, and positive characters show a typical readiness to put the needs and well-being of others ahead of their own. Associated with such unselfishness is courage. Richards' characters, though not unmindful of physical danger, are characteristically brave when bravery is required in a good cause. Most good causes involve protection of family, friends, children (regardless of origin), and the community as a whole. It is characteristic of Richards' fiction that heroic actions are usually performed by individuals who appear to be unheroic by conventional standards; and, generally, characters who are relatively uneducated and ill-at-ease in the mainstream of contemporary society are more likely to demonstrate heroic behavior than those who are more sophisticated. This is perhaps because heroism in Richards' characters still tends to be uncalculated, a projection of intrinsic individual merit.

Conventional success is much less important in Richards' fiction generally than are individual motives. And this is especially true of heroic behaviour, where it is impulse behind an action rather than outcome that determines whether the action is a hollow show of heroics or the genuine thing. True heroes of Richards' fiction are not the leaders – the queens of the hive – but the rank and file workers and soldiers, who, with no expectation of reward, are fated by their essential natures to perform heroically when duty demands it. For the most part, Richards' heroes are unaware that their bravery or self-sacrifice is anything special because it is so intrinsically a part of their being to behave heroically.

More than a few among those who have written on Richards' work have seen the lives it depicts as extremely bleak, if not downright hopeless. I see this view as resting on the assumption that Richards is, or ought to be, primarily interested in capturing a social milieu. This is not the case at all. It is the individual characters that are at the heart of Richards' creative commitment, and the focus of many critics on the conditions his characters face rather than their psychology, their values, and the spiritual resources they draw on in facing their conditions rests in too many cases on the idea that characters of a certain economic and educational background are better fitted to be the subjects of case studies than the protagonists of novels. But, again, success in the eyes of the world means little in Richards' novels, where virtue is its own reward.

This is partly because no other rewards are offered but more importantly because virtuousness entails expecting neither reward nor recognition. To miss this essential point is, like Christopher Wheem, the mean-spirited, self-serving English professor in *Hope in the Desperate Hour*, to fail to grasp the principle that some people at least exist "not to be comfortable but to be great."

What does the similarity between the subject of "Small Heroics" and the concerns of Richards' novels suggest? First, that Richards' work grows out of an imagined fictional world that is well worth understanding. This world, which is as much a creative representation of ideals as an attempt to record social conditions, has evolved as Richards has matured as a writer and thinker, but it nonetheless rests on fundamental values that were in place at the outset of his career. It suggests also that at the heart of Richards' achievement is a belief in and a fascination with the potential of human beings (and bees as well) for selfless, heroic sacrifice. Much has been made of Richards' ability to capture social and physical settings, and types of characters often neglected in fiction; too little recognition has been given to the philosophical and spiritual foundation on which his fictional world is constructed.

The Things of the Heart

INGE STERRER-HAUZENBERGER

On June 7th, 1988, looking out the window from a small room on the seventh floor of McLeod House on the UNB campus in Fredericton, I watched the sun coming out behind thousands of trees – sunrise over a dark sea. Later that day I would phone David Adams Richards to ask if I could come for a visit. His house was somewhere down there among those trees. This was to be the highlight of my visit to Canada, and I was nervous.

A few years earlier, Alden Nowlan's poetry was read at a guest talk at the University in Vienna where I was a student in the Department of English. David Richards had been mentioned. A young novelist from the same area as Nowlan, his name showed up on a list of Canadian writers suggested for M.A. theses. I looked forward to reading David Richards' novels because I liked Alden Nowlan's poems.

Blood Ties was the first of Richards' books to make it to our library in Vienna. Reading it gave me the feeling that I had found my book – and my writer. *Lives of Short Duration* left me deeply impressed, puzzled, touched to the heart, wanting to read more, ready to read it again.

That was the summer of 1987. The following year an Austrian scholarship allowed me to leave Vienna with all its lilacs in bloom and travel to a Canadian April of cold wind, snow, and rain in the city of Halifax. Lots of time to spend at Dalhousie University's Killam Library. I read and collected everything I could find about Richards' work, and found that the critical opinion was widely divergent. Everything from poor downtrodden violent people (society's losers) and ill-structured novels that went nowhere to comments about courage, compassion, self-sacrifice, human kindness, dignity, love, and forgiveness. It did not come as a surprise to see how divided the critics' reactions were – that tends to happen with great literature all over the world.

Gradually I began to see what for me as an Austrian was difficult to understand: Canadian critics did *not* want to have a great writer from the Maritimes; they did *not* want great novels set on a wild river. Regional prejudice, character and class prejudice, and the obsession to put Richards' work into the safe category of "regionalism" inhibited critics and reviewers from discovering the serious work of a great artist, and this prejudice thrust Richards' novels "outside" of the literary mainstream.

I began to understand that the Canadian literary

establishment, deeply entangled with the academic elite, didn't want to embrace a writer whose interest in the subjective experience and inner conflicts of his characters did not depend on sociological criteria but on "the things of the heart," on central values of humanity. The idea seemed to be that David Richards could be a fine writer if only he were sensible enough to write about different characters living different lives in different places.

There were people in Canada who seemed surprised that an Austrian, someone who lived 8000 miles away, was interested in the novels of a writer from "up there." The fascination for David Richards' books did not come from what critics often considered as "clear depictions of the working class in the small towns of New Brunswick," but from Richards' absolute reliance on subjectivity. He is a writer who has great compassion, sympathy, and respect for each of his characters. The thematic aspects of his novels are developed through the subjective experience of the characters, where everything is found in small details and not in theoretical explanations. Richards' respect for his characters ensures that there is never one authorial voice who knows "what it all means," nor is there ever one story *told* to the reader, but the consciousness of characters who find themselves in moments of physical or psychic crises are *shown*. These are the things – that reliance on "the things of the heart" – that touch me as a reader.

Later that June morning in 1988, I phoned David Richards and he invited me to his house for the afternoon. Was I supposed to interview him, to prepare questions, make notes, bring a tape recorder? I had no experience in talking to novelists – no idea at all save that I was writing a thesis on Richards' work. Grace, his lovely dog, received me as a friend, and so did David. That first visit became a story-telling afternoon with the best coffee west of Vienna. That afternoon was also the beginning of a dear and lasting friendship.

Later, when we walked by the river with Grace, I remembered to ask David about the last two words in *Lives of Short Duration*: "OIGOA/ Sepoitit."

"What does that mean?" Silence while we walked on.

Then he turned his head, looked at me, and smiled. "You are beautiful," he said. Very much surprised and flattered by this remark, I thought he hadn't heard my question.

"It's Micmac; you are beautiful, in Micmac," he explained, still smiling.

"Oh, who says it?" I managed to say, hoping he wasn't aware of my misinterpretation.

"I don't know," David said, "It's just there."

It's just there. The quiet beauty of uncalculating love, the beauty of human kindness. The compassion that becomes apparent at moments of crisis; it's this compassion that always brings out beauty. It's the beauty of spontaneous good will, the beauty of small gifts, of generosity, and of forgiveness. It's also the beauty of language, especially at moments when the subtle perceptions of characters reveal their innermost feelings.

The beauty of Richards' art is just there. It's created by the moral integrity of characters who try to come to terms with painful memories, with moments of failure, with guilt. This integrity is never a question of wealth, sophistication, luck, or social acceptance. It's a quality of human greatness that any of the characters can achieve or fall short of.

There is beauty and there is greatness in David's books, and anyone can find it who reads them not only with the eyes but also with the heart. His work still awaits a serious analysis both in Canada and abroad – there is so much yet to discover.

By the end of June I left Fredericton, where I had spent wonderful Canadian summer days with David, Peggy, and Grace. There had been long hours of storytelling. I remember the taste of salmon, mussels, and smoked oysters, and I will never forget that impressive wild river, the Miramichi. Ever since then, Richards' novels have been a part of my life.

Academics and Mavericks

FRED COGSWELL

Since World War ll I have read widely and thought much about contemporary Canadian prose and poetry. Both of these activities have reinforced my original impression that a grouping of Canadian writers in our time could be classified in two ways. I call one academic; the other maverick.

Both groups take writing seriously; both have written well technically, but the gulf between them, it seems to me, is not well enough understood. Academic writers tend to be those who discovered that good students can do well in a world of words by learning from their teachers and the books that these teachers recommend. In fact, many such, although they call themselves writers, spend most of their time and thought and receive most of their income by teaching others to learn to read and think as they have learned to read and think. It is not surprising, therefore, that their foremost thought process is analysis. The goal of analysis is understanding, and action is relegated to a secondary function. "To understand all is to forgive all" becomes a comforting doctrine since it requires no action other than an ongoing process that feeds on itself and no doubt can be led to justify anything.

Hence, the rift between the "civilized" thought of the modern world and the unspeakable barbarity of its conduct. Despite its cleverness and quality, I am continually depressed by reading the products of modern Academics. I prefer mavericks.

Among modern Canadian mavericks, I put such writers as the late Earle Birney and Alden Nowlan, and the still-living Raymond Souster, Irving Layton, Leonard Cohen, Al Purdy, Alistair MacLeod, Ray Fraser, Ray Smith, and, of course, David Adams Richards.

Most of these writers did not go to school for marks. In fact, most of them did not look for an academic education any longer than they had to because at a very early time in their lives they discovered what they wanted to do, which was to write. They discovered that they wanted to write because the best of the writers they read opened up their imaginations to worlds that they desired more than the ones in which they found themselves. They also discovered that the things they had been taught mattered far less than a well-imagined situation or character that could live in the mind by transference, through empathy. So their reading became a springboard for experiences they made their very own. By reading the Bible, Lao Tse, Dickens, Dostoevsky, Hugo, Twain, they became intelligently alive and passed that intelligent life on to all who read them and had wit enough to see their accomplishments.

"The poetry of earth is never dead," wrote John Keats, and as long as earth maintains its mavericks, among whom David Adams Richards is an important one, it cannot die – for mavericks are those driven to create "for the sake of a fine thing made."

Women in Richards' World

FRANCES MACDONALD

David Adams Richards writes about women the way
Henry James saw them: as persons, rather than as
women. There are others who write, as Richards
does, about drunks, sluts, heroes, and fools as persons, but to expose the hidden weaknesses and
strengths of women in the casual way that Richards
habitually does is a courageous act, and it is what I
admire most in his art.

Richards' world can be a scary place for readers
who didn't grow up in it, and a scarier one for those
who did. "Dysfunctional" is a word that could be
used as a bookmark in any Richards novel, and I'm
sure there are readers who feel that if he were any
kind of responsible author, he would send most of
his characters off for a few weeks in a good program somewhere. His people often make bad choices, ones that cause harm or misery to themselves or
others. And scariest of all is that the women are no
better than the men. But they are no worse than the
men, either: Richards pays women the respect of
not assuming that they *should* be better than men.

His women make unauthorized choices, and are
presented living with and through the consequences
of their choices, with no excuse or apology made

for them. Rita, in *Nights Below Station Street*, acknowledges to her daughter that she didn't love Joe when she married him, but does now. Marrying a man because he wants you, and learning to love him for it, is a survival technique inherited from the thousands of generations of women who had little choice in marriage or much else.

Nevertheless, no matter how restricted their lives were, women as well as men have always made choices from what limited options were available to them, choices which made sense to them, no matter how irrational they may have appeared to their neighbours, or to their great-grandchildren. In *Evening Snow Will Bring Such Peace* there is a woman who leaves her children with her husband and his parents to live with a more prosperous man. She is not a very likable character, malicious, complaining, familiar. But she survives, and so do her children. In *Hope in the Desperate Hour* there is a woman who gets herself and her family into all kinds of messes through her weakness and gullibility; she is not merely a victim of smarter and more ruthless people, she collaborates in her own downfall because she believes what she wants to believe. One of the things she wants to believe is that large sums of money are likely to fall into her hands through no effort on her part. She fights her way out of her troubles without necessarily understanding what went wrong, other than her luck. We might wish these women had more sense, or courage, or integrity, but they don't, and the world doesn't fall apart because they don't.

The inhabitants of Richards' world are an endangered species – rural survivors whose habitat is under siege from the dominant urban, middle class culture of the centre. Like the porcupines and raccoons who inhabit city parks and forage in the gardens and garbage cans of their human neighbours, Richards' people are adapting to the modern world, but most of them still live in pockets of wilderness, little mill towns and fishing or logging villages where the essential way of life *seems* unchanged. In their world, everyone knows how they are connected to everyone else, or if they don't know, the neighbours do and aren't telling. Their communities are tightly knit and well-darned, and people survive by helping each other out. Such communities are characterized by a sense of shared history, identity, and purpose. People know where they fit in, and conformity to the mores and conventions of the community is seen as important both for the individual and the community itself. Dissent is destructive, because if people can't get along and work together, survival becomes more difficult for everyone.

The dark side of closely knit communities is coercion by shame – the threat of losing status as a respectable member of the community is a powerful behaviour modifier, especially if the consequences of bad behaviour are held before your eyes. Richards is very good on the ways respectable people collaborate to keep the fallen from getting back on their feet, if only by assuming they won't or can't. We need falling down drunks and fallen women to serve as examples to keep each other in line.

Women, in Richards' world and elsewhere, are skilled practitioners of this kind of social control. Terrorism is the weapon of the powerless. The malicious whispering and targeting for ostracism among adolescent girls, which Richards treats seriously, is a shadow and foreshadow of the terrorism by which respectable women have protected their tenuous position in misogynist societies by differentiating themselves from dissident women. In Richards' world, you probably aren't going to get much help dealing with problems that characterize you as an outcast, problems seen as ones you brought on yourself.

Adele, the young girl in *Nights Below Station Street*, know this all too well. She conceals her pregnancy until her labour begins, and events are taken out of her hands. In everyone's best interest, she is persuaded to give her baby to a respectable woman who covets it, a "decision" she regrets the rest of her life. Two fundamental facts of life for women are the threat of having children, and the threat of losing them.

People who live their lives outside their community's conventions of respectability – through poverty, illness, ignorance, or dissent – frequently have as a fixture in their lives, a "worker," the sight of whose car can instill a shadow of the same fear provoked by the sight of a black car in distant streets where state terrorism is more brutal and more readily recognizable: they can both take your children away. Forty or fifty years ago, when the social agencies charged with managing the unsuccessful were run and staffed almost exclusively by men, the threat of having your children taken from you was relatively simple. If you were destitute, your children were taken and fed and housed elsewhere.

With the entrance into this and most other professional fields of large numbers of women, the rules changed, becoming more humane and balanced, but also more complex and elusive. The impulse to help and comfort even among women can also cover a need to exercise or acquire power and control. Altruism is seldom unmixed. In *Evening Snow*, a woman volunteers as a friendly visitor in the hospital, a laudable and charitable action. But one of the effects of her presence is to displace an old man's family at his bedside, rendering problematic any chance of reconciliation among those who had suffered through his long life with him. The sick old man naturally prefers the company of the cheerful stranger, even if she is a little nosy.

One of Richards' most powerful and controversial characters is Vera, the social worker, whose actions and beliefs are largely governed by her apparently unrecognized need to differentiate her own life from her mother's. Vera writes a book about the opposite sex that is meant to be taken seriously: a study of male violence, using Jerry Bines' life as an example. In doing so, she exercises a power that has traditionally been reserved for men, and does no better with it – she misunderstands, misrepresents, and dismisses Jerry's life, and by extension the lives of other men.

Richards, by writing about persons and situations as he sees them, without justifying or explaining them other than in their own terms, takes us a step or two farther along the road to a place and time when women and men can see and write about one another as distinct images, not distorted reflections.

Canada's Independent Intellectual

TONY TREMBLAY

One thing most graduate students in Canadian English classes know is Northrop Frye's oft-printed summation of Canadian literature, specifically that "There is no Canadian writer of whom we can say what we can say of the world's major writers, that their readers can grow up inside their work without ever being aware of a circumference" (*The Bush Garden* 214). Frye continues: "If no Canadian writer pulls away from the Canadian context toward the centre of literary expression itself, then at every point we remain aware of his social and historical setting" (214). Upon examination, Frye's two statements seem contradictory, not of each other but within themselves. Growing up inside of anything *requires* demarcation and periphery, for "inside" is understandable only if its opposite, "outside," is knowable, the opposite term's absence as meaningful as any presence. But the point is not to argue the theory willy nilly; rather, to test whether Frye's remarks about our literature are still valid as artistic measures. In my view, they never were; in my view, they reflect a colonial bias, the stigma of which remains entrenched in the Canadian ethos.

By extension, the inference that art should extinguish the particular for the universal seems ludicrous, the sort of pronouncement that cultural elitists like Eliot and Woolf were fond of making. Are readers of Faulkner and O'Connor not aware of Mississippi and Georgia; are readers of Hardy and Lawrence not aware of Wessex and Nottingham? Do Faulkner, O'Connor, Hardy, and Lawrence, the great regionalists, not occupy "the centre of literary expression?" What, then, limits "social and historical setting" from being a means to that centre? And what exactly admits the particularities of these great regionalists to universals?

In Frye's two statements, we witness what has been a sad truth about Canadian literature (and, indeed, Canadian culture) for the last century: the consensus, seeded and confirmed by our critics (Frye the greatest among them), that what is Canadian is second-rate. Eliot's fierce Anglophilia is but the blueprint that critics like Frye followed, critics who believe that for Canadian literature and art to evolve to a world stage it must cease being Canadian, must deny its "Canadian context." This, of course, as we know from Said, is the great lie of cultural imperialism, and it is a lie that Canada, wedged uneasily between two cultural monoliths (Britain and the U.S.A.), has ceded to. That we had little choice in the matter is noteworthy if inconsequential. The fact remains that Canadians have been rewarded for looking elsewhere for excellence in art, music, and literature – and that this "else-whereness," espoused by our second-greatest critic, Hugh Kenner, has informed the creation of art and literature in this country. Even critics from our own regions, none finer than Nova Scotia's R.J. MacSween, fell prey to this "elsewhere" envy. Assessing the world-class poet from New Brunswick, Alden Nowlan, MacSween wrote: "The only complaint from this reader is that Nowlan seems always to hunt in the territory which is already his own. It would be wonderful if he were to enter a land of volcanoes and wizards" (208). Volcanoes and wizards? There is not a volcano or wizard in Faulkner, O'Connor, Hardy, and Lawrence, all writers MacSween admired tremen-dously, all writers who hunt in territories of their very own. There is, however, a sense of "awayness" in their hinterlands, a sense that confers legitimacy by virtue of difference. While regions from away constitute literary landscapes, then, regions from home, if we are to believe the experts, rarely do.

I would be manipulative of the truth if I implied that the young Faulkner, O'Connor, Hardy, or Lawrence experienced anything different in their times. Fact is, they experienced much the same thing. Reeking of the familiar, their works were similarly dismissed. The foulest smells always seem to issue closest to home, at least in the estimation of home-bred critics.

*

At the university – the place where [Wheem] had staked his whole life – his amorality had become moral; and he had treasured this intellectual comfort. All of a sudden people were saying how moral, how comforting he was to women and he, in his three-piece suit, began to believe this also. It didn't matter if it was true. Only that it didn't have to be true if people believed it.

(*Hope in the Desperate Hour* 94)

*

I establish this bias as a way of introducing David Adams Richards, though I admit being uncomfortable in introducing a writer through the detritus of his critical reception. To appreciate Richards, however, is to understand something of that reception. Richards is unique in Canadian literature for the drubbing he has taken at the hands (and feet) of critics, the vast majority of whom have been urban, academic, and miles removed from the social periphery which Richards inhabits and explores. When I say Richards is unique, I mean he leads all other Canadian writers in the abuse he has taken. And when I say he inhabits and explores a social periphery, I mean to say that, as an Atlantic Canadian artist, he exists outside of the ideological engine-room of our nation, both culturally and politically. His sensibility is working class, rural, and anti-intellectual, the consequence of which has been his labelling as "literary regionalist" by critics and appraisers from away. But if Richards is a mere regionalist, then so is Chekhov; not a bad thing to be a regionalist, which is the secret we in the hinterlands are not telling, the secret that time alone will confer as excellence.

The reception of Richards' novel *Hope in the Desperate Hour* (1996) is indicative of what I am saying about his critical reception. The following reviews come from Canada's largest-circulating mainstream media – from *Maclean's* magazine, our national weekly, and from two of our most-read dailies, *The Montreal Gazette* and *The Globe and Mail*.

Entitled "Beautiful losers," the *Maclean's* review begins,

> . . . the novels of David Adams Richards are an acquired taste. One of the country's best writers, he is not among its most popular for the simple reason that his books are so often sad . . . [Richards] ferrets out the tragedy in the lives of marginal people. (24 June 1996)

The Montreal Gazette review, sinisterly entitled, "If not for dysfunction, these losers wouldn't function at all," also takes a personal affront to Richards' fictive cast and landscape, portraying the author again as a rat ferreting out misery in a human landfill:

> Like much of Richards's fiction, *Hope in the Desperate Hour* . . . assembles the usual collection of chronic losers and low-rent dreamers. When they aren't abusive,

they are unreliable . . . There are so many doomed
points of view drifting in and out of the narrative it may
be hard to find your way . . . You may also be tempted
to ask why you should bother. (25 May 1996)

The third review, from *The Globe and Mail*, starts
to sound familiar, a tawdry concord that has clear
ideological overtones:

> . . . a sky has lowered a storm and anyone who hasn't
> been afflicted by scandal, shame, rejection, marital col-
> lapse, police investigation or medical calamity is about
> to get their due . . . For desperation in this abundance,
> time isn't measure enough . . . [Richards sets a] standard
> for unsentimental observation of the blighted, eternally
> straitened lives of people trying to do right and ending
> up, most of them, wronged. In Richards' novels there's
> always some abstract smell in the air, 'of evening,' or 'of
> snow.' It's rank tragedy, more like . . . The promise of
> hope notwithstanding, the inevitability of despair hangs
> heavy. (20 April 1996)

The constant in the review segments above is a
direct and undisguised frontal attack against
Richards' working-class people (against the majority of New Brunswickers), an attack that, if mount-
ed outside the presumed "make-believe" world of
fiction, would bring the swiftest penalties imagina-
ble, those reserved for an enlightened "zero tolerance." Canada's new intellectualism holds, then,
and paradoxically, that we must empathize with the
working-class in real life, but in fiction, obviously,

we are free to despise them. (Does this discrepancy in tolerances say anything about enlightened attitudes? You bet it does!) The diction alone betrays the sour taste left in the mouths of the culturally elite who, in Richards' work, must suddenly contend, not at arm's length but face-to-face, with the recipients of their social welfare. To translate their prejudice, that which is presented as official mainstream verdict in our largest-circulating print media, Richards is not "popular" because his books are "sad," focusing on the "inevitability of despair"; he is not popular because he writes about the "marginal" – what *The Globe and Mail* reviewer patronizingly refers to as "the good people of New Brunswick"; and he is not popular because his characters are "losers" who "smell" bad and whose "dreams" are tantamount to "dysfunction." Such judgement, full of the prejudice of centre and privilege, smacks of the worst kind of colonial, satisfied dismissal. Yet it is tolerated; indeed, the sum of this criticism informs our national consciousness. And Richards, who has confronted these attitudes directly in his work, has paid the price accordingly.

If scorn alone were the only criteria for greatness, Richards would be our greatest writer. However, when scorn as critical reception is added to the remarkable quantity and quality of his literary output, Richards has no equals in Canada; he *is* our greatest writer, for whom scorn is a reflection, albeit twisted, of the freshness of his vision. So precocious is that vision that critics, who sense their own tolerances and ideals being challenged, respond to his work with anxiety and rancour. And just as Henry James and F.R. Leavis, the greatest critics of Hardy's time, dismissed the "poor little" Dorsetshire writer not only as "factitious and insubstantial" (James 28) but so insignificant as to hardly bear mentioning in *The Great Tradition*, so have Canadian critics dismissed Richards, pushing him outside of what has been deemed the safe and proper sphere of literary attention. In both cases (for Hardy and Richards), it is anxiety, discomfort, and awe expressed as dismissal. As I have written elsewhere, Richards is the most admired and berated and misunderstood Canadian writer of the century.

Humans are savage in the absence of precedent. Thus, our most celebrated artists are rarely championed in their lifetimes; instead, veneration usually goes to the popular, as two of the three Richards reviewers above openly admit.

*

It felt good to be in the hayfield again. The day was hot. Across the river the reserve sat blinded in the heat. The slanted roofs, the smoke from the far-off dump. A dry road led through its centre, and now and then a car silently travelled that road. In the late afternoon he went down to the river to sit and drink a bottle of beer. A salmon rolled in the rip just out from him.

(*Hope in the Desperate Hour* 46)

*

Though I have chosen – again, with reservation – to enter Richards' work through the fallout of his critical reception, I now move from effect to cause, examining the raw material of Richards' artistic vision, that which has made the Canadian critical establishment so uncomfortable and defensive. To begin, Richards' literary output has established him as a writer who must be taken seriously; in fact, few Canadian writers in the last twenty-five years have been as prolific as Richards, who will publish his fourteenth book this fall. A related problem (the fundamental one as I see it) that Richards' work presents for the critical establishment is an unprecedented consistency of moral vision. His first published volume, a collection of poems entitled *Small Heroics* (1972), documents early in his writing career the concerns that dominate his mature work. In its title, the collection announces Richards' preoccupation with that which is outside the literary mainstream, whether it is "angered dogs / Who behind hedge rows / Bark at flakes" ("Barren Man") or old women who "Strain out excrement in pain / And think of tired things" ("An Old Woman"). Appearing next to what traditionally has been considered non-literary subject matter is also Richards' concern in this collection with the constancy of suffering. The "small heroics" of bees hopelessly but valiantly defending their hive against a human's extermination ("Small Heroics") is presented as on par with the inconsequence of human misery:

> There is a certain Harmless
> Walking on the road
> A beggar in the morning
> Wading spring water
> Collecting bottles as he goes;
>
> Before his time another
> Existed exactly the same
> Collected refuse in a ditch
> A wet sack making him lame.
>
> ("Traditional")

Though the subject matter of *Small Heroics* does not include the "volcanoes and wizards" that for some constitute appropriate literary attention, the feel for emotional suffering, lived experience, and the resilience of the human spirit in Richards' first published work is remarkable, especially when one considers that he was only twenty-two when the collection appeared. Such precocity, as Dylan Thomas's self-destructive boozing confirmed, is always a dangerous thing, both to its host and to those subjects it implicates in its gaze.

*

You do not always know how things happen. They just do, and then in hindsight and with reflection, you have

the feeling of an epiphany – of some kind of justice in
the faintest measure in all things, all events.

(*Hope in the Desperate Hour* 27)

*

From the time of his first published volume of
poems and first fictional trilogy, Richards' work has
focused both on the downtrodden and on the
motives of so-called liberal humanist interventions
to alleviate suffering. Whether disenfranchised or
empowered, his characters are good and bad, heroic and cowardly, spontaneous and calculating, their
deeds and actions often speaking in opposition to
what they are allowed to think of themselves. The
reckless John Delano in *The Coming of Winter* is a
good example of this incongruity between actions/
instincts and words. Dismissed as self-serving by
most of the characters in the novel (and, indeed,
most of the readers looking into it), John struggles
throughout the narrative not so much to come to
terms with the accidental death of his best friend,
but to find a way of providing for his best-friend's
girlfriend, who is left pregnant and alone in the
wake of the tragedy. What actually happens as a
result of John's struggle is less important than the
struggle itself, which is manifest as a fuzzy abstrac-
tion in John's unconscious mind. Booze and his
own worst tendencies only defer a resolve that his
instincts and his loyalty to his dead friend cannot
deny: "He kept glancing from side to side as he

drank but more often glancing up the road toward her place, her home as if he knew in himself he must see her now" (128).

Such subtlety of intentions is what characterizes Richards' work, giving it the power that only a disciplined and spare fidelity to truth can convey. What Richards is interested in exploring is not a showy, angst-ridden emotionalism but the quiet insecurities, perplexities, and loyalties that constitute a life. Many times his characters admit that *they* don't even know the reasons for their own actions, as Arnold does in *Road to the Stilt House* when he says "I can never tell you why I got the tattoo on my back. I never know why I smell gritty stove dirt in my blood, or why I falsely told the RCMP officer I blamed Canada for my own lost mistakes" (89). Equally perplexed by his own motives, Joe Walsh, too, is paralyzed by the same kind of uncertainty:

> The worst of it was that he had no faith in himself concerning this [job]. If he did not do the job he would be looked upon as ridiculous. If he looked ridiculous perhaps Rita would think it was because he had quit drinking and had gone strange. If he did not do it he would feel less than himself, and yet, once he had done it, he felt something would happen that could make him regret it.
>
> (*Nights Below Station Street* 154)

The outcome of Joe's dilemma, like the outcome of

John and Arnold's (like the outcome of Tracy McCaustere's in *Hope in the Desperate Hour*) is not the focus of Richards' effort. Instead, the allowance for uncertainty that Richards gives his characters is a passport to their freedom – to succeed or fail on their own, without their creator's intervention. And, usually, the stakes are not as spectacular as success or failure; usually, the stakes are much more subtle: struggling to overcome personal weakness and fear, confronting the private demons of alcohol and violent upbringing, and battling the various attitudes that seed inferiority. As Sheldon Currie writes, the kind of subtlety of the unconscious that Richards employs, as well as the personal agency he gives his characters, is not the stuff of popular fiction, nor is it for the faint of heart:

> All Richards' work requires close attention, a healthy tolerance for ambiguity, and an ability to get along without cheap novelistic tricks: silly sex, needless violence, fashionable ideas, *au courant* dialogue, and romanticized characters. And more than anything else the reader needs to bring the kind of intelligence and imagination necessary to discover meaning without the author's intervention, as well as the wit and sense of humour to see the comic in the tragic and vice versa; these are troubled waters, these Miramichi River stories, complex and profound, simultaneously comic and tragic, [not] for the inexperienced or the inattentive . . . (67-68)

That Richards' imagined world takes work (in the

form of concentration) and a good deal of lived experience (in the form of emotional maturity) admits his art to the realm of the serious, where manner and motive, humour and compassion, attain spiritual dimension. And though he has evolved technically from his first fictional trilogy, Richards is rare in that his aesthetic emerged fully formed. The combination of Richards' high moral seriousness and what he assumes to be his reader's commitment, in kind, to his exploration of the triumphs and absurdities of the human heart, removes his work from a popular ground. Inattentive readers, as Currie correctly suggests, can easily miss the point.

*

His father would stand with his shirt out weaving back and forth, his right fist cocked a little, back against the wall, and the dry earth, the smell of hay, tumbling with the crickets and the smell of summer and all the world jostling in trumpets of song – a mentally unfit melancholy man along a road with a little boy by the hand. Then you know truth. You don't know it before then. (This is what he could not tell Vera, of course.) You don't know it before then.

(*For Those Who Hunt the Wounded Down* 79)

*

A lack of compromise to the sloth of contemporary tolerances is only one aspect of, and actually incidental to, Richards' work, even though that sloth is writ large in his critical reception. Much more deliberate in Richards' programme is a preoccupation with the social constructions of normalcy. Consequently, his work often challenges and interrogates what we as educated, middle-class readers assume to be "normal" and "expected," with the result usually being the private admission that our assumptions are not only false but damaging to those they implicate. To read Richards carefully, then, is to be constantly surprised into self-discovery and reassessment, exactly those discoveries that we as educated moderns like the least.

Richards' treatment of the presumably delinquent Jerry Bines in *Road to the Stilt House* and later in *For Those Who Hunt the Wounded Down* provides abundant evidence of the surprise of subverted expectation. When he is introduced in the first novel, Bines is a small-town thug, ruthlessly preying upon the defenceless Arnold, whose fear of Bines is focused on "coarse and steel-toed" boots that he'd seen "kick a wounded deer to death" (40). Implicated in the theft of jewelry and clothing from the churchyard vault, suspected in the murder of a Norwegian sailor, and given to terrorizing Arnold at will, Bines has little to redeem him in the first novel in which he appears, except the brief suggestion at the end that he is a fulfillment of others' worst fears:

The police did no favours for Jerry Bines, and he did no

favours for them. It started long ago with the police.
They did no favours for him, for a long time. When he
went to jail . . . they knew he was a bad apple. They
knew that from day one, and treated him accordingly.
One day led to the next and soon he was being locked
up during exercise. Soon he was let out of his cell only
to shower.

(*Stilt House* 166)

Leaving only that unexplored suggestion that Bines
is not the sole author of his fate, Richards closes the
novel with a promise that "The road, sooner or
later, will tell us everything. We only have to wait"
(*Stilt House* 171). And so, like Arnold, who also
knows the truth that the road will tell (118), we
wait, a wait that is almost ten years. Two other novels are published, a new trilogy cemented. Bines
reappears in the final book of that trilogy, in *For
Those Who Hunt the Wounded Down*, his presence
held in abeyance as if to challenge the casual reader's
span of attention (as if, as well, to show critics like
Frye that it *is* possible to grow up inside his fiction).

    When Bines is again introduced, he is attended
by all the fabulous rumour and gossip of a bad reputation, and we, safe like the townsfolk in the
novel, revel in his badness: that "he was the only
man to ever come over the wall at Dorchester"
(*Wounded* 8); that he was "the kind of man who if
he can't beat you with his fist would get a brick"
(25). Catching us unaware, however, are a series of
less fantastic insights about Bines that only frag-

ments reveal: his love of children, his protection of
the innocent, his forgiveness of human weakness,
his tenderness toward a sick son, and, most remark-
ably, his genuine desire for reform. When we exit
the subterfuge of communal myth-making and gossip and enter Bines' own consciousness, we discover a personality and spirit that our expectations cannot accommodate. But Richards doesn't let us off
that easily. To further unsettle our assumptions
about the tidiness of character and class, Richards
introduces a foil for Bines, a personality whose
well-intentioned, middle-class motives mirror our
own. A social worker specializing in child welfare,
Vera is a character we recall from an earlier novel,
Nights Below Station Street. As her introduction in
Nights indicates, she is rather hapless and pathetic,
given to trends and low self-worth:

> Vera was tall and thin, and she wore a pair of granny
> glasses with golden frames and big long flowery dress-
> es . . . Vera had affected a sort of British accent from a
> year at Oxford . . . As a little girl Vera had read all of
> Jane Austen. She began writing poems, and they had a
> poetry group at noon hour in the school. She was inter-
> ested in all kinds of things. (Nevin [her boyfriend] had-
> n't read anything but because he grew a beard everyone
> assumed he had.) Vera always seemed to be alone.
> Ralphie would watch her coming up the lane, as a
> schoolgirl carrying her books in her arms, with her big
> round glasses fogged up and snow falling on her hair.
> Because she always ate oranges the boys used to call
> her sucker. And she was always looking for new

friends. And there was a great deal of silence about her. (91-92)

When Vera reappears in *Wounded*, her motives, like Bines', are revealed. She has since divorced Nevin "for mental and emotional cruelty, and [speaks] calmly about this" (*Wounded* 22), and she seeks out Bines as a malleable ground for her pop psychologizing:

> It wasn't that his story interested her so much. But he fitted a pattern that she had concerned herself about over the last four or five years. And she had convinced herself that she could expose this pattern better than anyone else, show his kind of male violence, show the broader scope of such violence and how it "impacted" on children and women. "Impacted" being the new word of choice for her at this moment. (22-23)

When entered, Vera's own consciousness reveals a cold-hearted ideologue, whose covert and unreflexive violence is much more insidious than that ever carried out by Bines. What is remarkable about both characters is not the opposite path of their trajectories across three novels, but our own desire as middle-class readers to assign them qualities neither deserves: Bines doesn't deserve our condemnation any more than Vera deserves our admiration. In fact, opposite trajectories may not even exist; the more likely probability is that Bines always tended toward moral goodness and Vera toward moral corruption.

Quick to judge, however, we assume what we've be taught to assume. As Richards has written elsewhere, "If one of my characters had a car up on blocks in his back yard, he must be *illiterate*, and probably *slept* with his sister" ("My Miramichi Trilogy" 78).

What is at stake in Richards' later work, then, is a wholesale examination of the motives and perceptions of liberal humanism, especially when "impacting upon" interventions to alleviate the suffering of the downtrodden. Why is it, Richards is asking, that progressive ideology as active, often disruptive, intervention goes unquestioned? Why is it that enlightened attitudes and their attendant "isms" pass for models of social justice? Why is it that the educated middle-class suddenly has a monopoly on social concern, and that social concern is immediately assumed to be the hallowed (and non-partisan) business of a few? As Father Billy says at the close of *Road to the Stilt House*: "'Meddling has killed them, legislation has destroyed their house; how can anyone be legislated to have honour, to love or hope for goodness, when there is triumph in the social worker's face and pride in the schoolmaster's eyes?'" (158). The result of such narrow and self-serving attitudes, Richards' illustrates, is a further hunting of the already-wounded, and so Vera's eventual book on Bines, entitled *The Victims of Patriarchy (and Its Inevitable Social Results)*, is in the end not about Bines and how he "shook your hand" (51) but about Vera, just as all middle-class interventions ultimately serve the middle class. In telling truths about ideology that are not only unfashionable but that implicate those who have taken out student loans to pay for their moral positions, Richards has attracted the wrath of those who chart our ideological ground.

*

God calls on man not to be comfortable but to be great.
(*Hope in the Desperate Hour* 146)

*

If we are to marshal the evidence of Richards' assessment via the inference of his critics' wrath, we must not only conclude that his subject matter is deficient of literary merit and that his social satires unworthy of advanced ethics of correctness, but that the role of the artist in society is to affirm rather than interrogate social and ideological truth. Fortunately for all of us, Richards has dispelled these myths in his work, showing us an opposite way. But to suggest that his path has been easy would be to do him an injustice, for, like all great artists, he has not only had to deal with the lading of his genius but with the intolerance of those along the way. I have therefore called him in the subtitle of this article, Canada's "independent" intellectual, choosing C. Wright Mills' term as a descriptor.

Himself an uncompromising intellectual, Mills wrote the following about the responsibility of the intellectual in the twentieth century:

> The independent artist and intellectual are among the few remaining personalities equipped to resist and to fight the stereotyping and consequent death of genuinely lively things. Fresh perception now involves the capacity continually to unmask and to smash the stereotypes of vision and intellect with which modern communications swamp us. (299)

Along with only a handful of other writers and public intellectuals in our mass-society, Richards is worthy of Mills' highest calling.

Robertson Davies wondered aloud in the first book of his Deptford trilogy whether or not Canadians would recognize a saint if one were presented to them through selfless action. Based on the neglect of Mary Dempster, his saint in *Fifth Business,* he concluded that we would not. In David Adams Richards, Davies' hunch is again confirmed – mind you, not because Richards is any kind of saint, but because his books, which are modern-day morality plays, have been systematically neglected and dismissed. I say "systematically" to reflect both what has gone on and what Richards has identified as the calculation of dismissal as opposed to the spontaneousness of good will.

As Walker Percy has written, it is rare that adults are treated to a fresh vision; it is rare that they can recapture "the loss of the creature" (46). Well, to read Richards is to read so outside the literary mainstream, that reading him is to read again for the first time. As John Moss has observed,

> It is difficult to imagine prose more elliptical and precise . . . Richards writes with such integrity, in ways sanctioned . . . not by precedent or convention but by an utter conviction in the truth of what he does, that the genius of his art makes . . . a vision of the human condition that excites and appalls with stunning force (298).

In an age of abundant confusion over morality – an age in which, writes Richards, many mistake "being nice for being good, being compliant for taking a moral stand" ("Remembering My Evaluators" 13) – the fiction of David Adams Richards takes considerable risks in documenting the only kind of truths which have (and will) outlive sophistry: truths of charitable intention, of self-sacrifice, of courageous action, of humility, and of that fierce human capacity to remain hopeful, often against all the evidence and all the odds. Though some critics, I am ashamed to admit, have shown little tolerance for anything but new-age morality in their literature, many readers, distrusting the critical establishment, are starting to take a second look at a writer whose quantity and quality of literary production is unmatched in Canada today.

David Adams Richards is one of our best-kept

cultural secrets. He won't be for long. If ever there has been a Canadian writer whose body of work and constancy of human care deserve Nobel consideration, Richards qualifies. His life's work has been the documentation of a pure and simple spiritualism. The lifeblood of a people has been his sacred trust. Many have grown up inside his work, delighted by the familiar and knowing with certainty that someday soon the fictional Miramichi will be as well known as Yoknapatawpha. It is certainly as richly conceived and presented, as carefully cherished and protected.

WORKS CITED

Currie, Sheldon. "David Adams Richards: The People on the Roadway." *The Antigonish Review*. 99 (Autumn 1994): 67-75.

Davies, Robertson. *Fifth Business*. Toronto: Macmillan, 1970.

Frye, Northrop. *The Bush Garden: Essays on the Canadian Imagination*. Toronto: Anansi, 1971.

James, Henry. "Review of *Far From the Madding Crowd*." *Nation* (24 December 1874). In *Thomas Hardy: The Critical Heritage*. R.G. Cox, Ed. London: Routledge & Kegan Paul, 1970.

Kenner, Hugh. *The Elsewhere Community*. Concord, Ontario: Anansi, 1998.

MacSween, R.J. "R.J. MacSween Special Issue." *The Antigonish Review*. 87-88 (Fall 1991/Winter 1992).

Mills, C. Wright. "The Social Role of the Intellectual." *Power, Politics and People: The Collected Essays of C. Wright Mills*. Irving Louis Horowitz, Ed. New York: Oxford University Press, 1963. 292-304.

Moss, John. *A Reader's Guide to the Canadian Novel*. 2nd Ed. Toronto: McClelland and Stewart, 1987.

Percy, Walker. "The Loss of the Creature." *The Message in the Bottle*. 1954. New York: Farrar, Straus and Giroux, 1987. 46-63.

Richards, David Adams. *The Coming of Winter*. Ottawa: Oberon Press, 1974.

——. *For Those Who Hunt the Wounded Down*. Toronto: McClelland & Stewart, 1993.

——. *Hope in the Desperate Hour*. Toronto: McClelland & Stewart, 1996.

——. "My Miramichi Trilogy: A Practising Novelist's View of the Novel in New Brunswick." Published Proceedings of the *6th International Literature of Region and Nation Conference*. 1998. Vol. II, 73-84.

——. *Nights Below Station Street*. Toronto: McClelland & Stewart, 1988.

——. "Remembering My Evaluators While Packing to Leave Home." *Pottersfield Portfolio* 19.1 (Fall 1998): 11-16.

——. *Road to the Stilt House*. Ottawa: Oberon Press, 1985.

——. *Small Heroics*. Fredericton: The New Brunswick Chapbooks, No. 17. 1972.

David Adams Richards for the New Millennium

1998. In two years we'll take down our Christmas trees and put away our baubles and drop the 20th century into a big brown box and ship it off to the museum of "time gone by" where historians can dig into it and deconstruct and reconstruct, recreating history, herstory, itstory, ourstory, and theirstory, valiantly trying to rescue bits and pieces of our ancestors from oblivion. Sometime in the 21st century, after the sun burns off the fog, literary historians will discover bright and shining in their field of vision, David Adams Richards, the most important Canadian novelist of this now-spent century. Other stars will still shine in the sky, but will be visible only at night, when the sun dips for a time below the horizon.

Extravagant claim? Well, we'll see. There are only two categories to consider. The quality of the writing and the quantity of the writing. If it were only a question of the quality it would be a hard choice for consistently beautiful prose between Alistair MacLeod, Alice Munro, Mavis Gallant, and David Adams Richards. But when it comes to qual-

ity *and* quantity combined in the novel, Richards
has no equal.

We have plenty of novelists who enjoy critical
and popular success. Richards' work will never be
popular because he makes no concession to the general reader's inability to fathom a subtle sentence,
nor does he cede an inch to fashion; indeed, he is
more apt to mock than to suffer the innumerable
injustice collectors, special pleaders, and black or
whites among us. His love for his unlikely heroes is
as palpable as rancid 999, but like Dylan Thomas,
he does not expect them to be *au courant*, and certainly not literate, nor sporting a good score on the
latest survey of mores.

> I write
> On these spindrift pages
> . . . for the lovers, their arms
> Round the griefs of the ages,
> Who pay no praise or wages
> Nor heed my craft or art.

Richards' novels will never be popular because they
require of the reader a surrender of the imagination
few are willing to risk, but for those few the reward
is an infinite awareness of a previously unknown
world. After reading for a week in Richards'
Miramichi a reader feels the need to unpack a set of
luggage, launder the dirty clothes, and take a shower.

Although I have been reading David Adams
Richards' work for years, and lived two years in his

country along the Miramichi River, I met him only once and spoke to him for only a few moments. He was reading earlier this year to an auditorium full of appreciative students and faculty from several of his books, including a delightful passage from *Hockey Dreams: Memoirs of a Man Who Couldn't Play*, a book not very well done by his editors, but which I enjoy anyway because I agree with so much of what is in it. His reading of it was superb and delighted the audience. For some reason or other, during the question period, also very entertaining, interesting, and instructive, he got inspired either by the audience or by himself to defend himself against the charge of being a merely regional writer.

What a surprise. I thought that foolishness was over. When somebody says someone is a regional writer it usually means the writer comes from the wrong region. Faulkner was a regional writer until Jean-Paul Sartre discovered him and suddenly Oxford, Mississippi became more than a local habitation and a name. Flannery O'Connor was a regional writer until she found an intelligent editor with an imagination and suddenly Milledgeville, Georgia became the center of a universe. But how many people these days, other than captive students and their jailers, read *Absolom, Absolom* or *Wise Blood*? On the other hand, someone will always be reading them; whereas soon, no one will be reading what everybody is reading now. London is a region in England, New York is a region in the United

States, Toronto is a region in Canada, and of course books about places like that attract readers. If you want to be popular, don't leave your heart in Tabusintac, leave it in San Francisco, and get Tony Bennett to cry your pain. But in the future, Oxford, Miss., Milledgeville, Ga., and Miramichi, N.B. will be the capital cities of the only kind of regions that matter in the fiction country. W.H. Auden said it well: "A poet's hope: to be / like some valley cheese / local, but prized elsewhere."

Laughs in the Desperate Hour

HERB WYILE

When I was starting my Ph.D. at the University of New Brunswick, I lived around the corner from David Richards (who I had met while writing a Master's thesis on his work) and on my occasional visits had the great benefit of David and his wife Peggy's hospitality and some of David's many stories. I remember one in particular, about a reading he gave, in northeastern New Brunswick I believe, which serves nicely by way of introduction to my topic here – the humour of his work. The reading, which had contained some swearing, was followed by a pronounced silence, after which a matronly member of the audience proceeded to chastise him. "Mr. Richards," he was told, "the only four-letter word we use around here is L-O-V-E" (this, David later pointed out, in an area with a long history of sectarian hostility and conflict). He recounted this unappreciative reception of his work not with annoyance but with a characteristic warmth and humour, qualities which also make his work as rich and enduring as it is.

You wouldn't know it, though, judging by the

general tenor of critical responses to Richards' work. His fictional territory is described as relentlessly grim and sombre, marked by unemployment, violence, alcoholism, and poverty, and deprived of light, hope, and human sympathy. W. H. New typifies this kind of reception in his *A History of Canadian Literature* (1989) in writing that, "in the dour works set in the Miramichi," Richards "portrays a world where individuals are powerless to escape the numbing effects of the community in which they live, an angry world where the lack of opportunity and the lack of language confirm each other . . ." (235).

For a writer whose first book, *The Coming of Winter*, opens with Kevin Dulse, caught up in the prospect of bagging a deer, but shooting a cow by mistake, such an emphasis is off the mark. Rather, I think that, given Richards' reputation and his already sizable body of work, one thing that still needs to be emphasized is how funny a writer he is. Now, a Richards novel is never going to be mistaken for a comic romp, and you'll have to get fairly far down into any review before you'll find the word "funny," but all the same, Richards' fiction is much more consistently humorous than it gets credit for.

The humour in Richards' work starts with his protagonists, most of whom tend to be social outcasts moving in and out of scrapes with their families, with representatives of social institutions, and with more socially empowered characters, and they have a certain picaresque quality. The central characters of his early work in particular, such as Orville in *Blood Ties*, Arnold in *Road to the Stilt House*, and John Delano in the first two novels, along with Adele of *Nights Below Station Street*, are characterized by a frustrated energy and desire that often lead to comic situations. Arnold's battles with the rest of his household often have their comic side, for instance when he reacts to his discovery that his mother's boyfriend Harry has been sending her money into a gospel program by kicking in the family television. In the process, he cuts his brother's face and sets his shoe on fire. Adele's strained relationship with Joe is full of comic moments, such as when Joe falls asleep with a burning cigarette and sets his pants on fire, and Adele reacts by throwing a bucket of water not on his pants but in his face; there's also the scene in which Adele, who's having her period, comes home from school to find the only two tea bags in the house – which she needs "because it stabilizes my system, up and down, so there you go" (111) – are on Joe's eyes, because he's been temporarily blinded during a welding job. When he lifts one to look at her she snatches it and runs off. For me, though, the figure who stands out as Richards' foremost comic achievement is the irrepressible Little Simon Terri of *Lives of Short Duration*, whose cheerful defiance and genius for practical jokes give a lot of spark to the novel. His

run-ins with the RCMP are particularly memorable:
when they haul him in and strip-search him, con-
vinced they've finally caught him red-handed smug-
gling drugs, Simon says "Ke-rist boys – jus cause I
come from a poor family . . . How many times ya
wanta look at me little nob anyways?" (240), and
when they quiz him about carrying a baseball bat in
his car he says "I don't know where it come from –
it wasn't there las weekend. Oh Jesus yes, yes I give
Hank Aaron a lift – " (240). This kind of comedy of
the underdog is definitely a Richards specialty.

While Richards' work has little of the stylized,
often ironic wit of a lot of humorous writing, his
dialogue is consistently humorous, and many of his
characters display a great deal of verbal energy,
quirkiness, and punch. Richards' work is full of
evocative turns of phrase like "busy as a cake at a
wake," "the goddamn baboon arse," and "ya have-
ta half beg him to do anything," and many of his
characters are, in their own inimitable fashion,
humorously eloquent. Indeed, one of the most
prevalent misconceptions about Richards' characters, next to the view that their lives are unremit-
tingly bleak, is that they are inarticulate – a conclusion based on the assumption that being articulate
means being verbally sophisticated. While a good
many of Richards' characters may at times be reti-
cent or self-conscious about expressing themselves,
they're certainly not incapable of it. When Joe says
to Adele after she is caught shoplifting, "Zellers

wasn't made to keep the likes of you in panty-hose"
(72), the point is pretty clear – and pretty funny.
The same goes for Little Simon's observation that
"guilt . . . is always with ya – can't go a day without
sneezin in the wrong Kleenex" (214) or Old
Simon's response, upon being told of Ceril Brown's
complaints about Indians: "Ceril Brown should
shut his mouth about the Indian . . . He'd a died
eatin his own shit if it weren't for Daniel Ward, the
time he got lost" (*Lives* 97). While the thought
might require some readjustment on the part of
Canadian readers seasoned on a diet of Margaret
Atwood and Robertson Davies, the language of
Richards' characters is vivid, vital, and humorous,
and not the stunted utterings of blighted souls.

Another reason readers might not be inclined to
think of Richards as a humorous writer is that so
much of his humour is situational. A perfect example is the scene in *Lives of Short Duration* in which
Old Simon Terri's daughter-in-law Devoda, in a
condescending gesture of misplaced and contrived
compassion, ushers mourners out of the room so
that he can have a last moment with his wife
Merium, and Old Simon, self-conscious and at a
loss as to what is expected of him, simply nods at
the corpse after several minutes and leaves. In *Road
to the Stilt House*, the chronically unemployed
Arnold gets a job holding a traffic sign on a highway
crew and gets an unwelcome visit from his younger
brother Randy, whose presence embarrasses Arnold

in front of the rest of the crew; Randy then delivers the *coup de grâce* by leaving his leftover lunch for Arnold in a bucket with Goofy and Pluto on it and "the rest of the evening that crazy bucket with the picture of Goofy and Pluto looked at Arnold, and sized him up" (83). It's not the kind of humour that will crack 'em up at parties, but it's a constant presence in Richards' work that belies the description of his writing as relentlessly grim and depressing.

Having said that, though, it's important to recognize that if Richards' writing is humorous, most of that humour is of the dark variety. Some of the more grotesque images from *Lives*, for instance, are also some of the funniest: George Terri parading around with a pig's head impaled on a stick at a party celebrating his daughter's Atlantic Loto win, and Lester Murphy disguised in a pumpkin head and suit, trying to set fire to his own tavern to cash in on the insurance. This ambivalence is true even of *Road to the Stilt House*, perhaps Richards' starkest and yet most lyrical book, where the internecine warfare between Arnold's family and Sadie and Harry not only swings in intensity and alliances but also keeps the brutal and the comic in close proximity. When Sadie hauls Randy by the hair into the kitchen and forces him to drink a glass of dirty dishwater, Arnold meekly protests, "Isn't that enough? He'll begin to bloat up" (22). Later, when Arnold, who has vowed not to trust the police, is beaten up by his nemesis Jerry Bines and the RCMP arrive to interview him, he hides in a closet while the rest of the household gleefully contributes to his humiliation:

> "There's been no fights here," Sadie said.
>
> "No fights," Mabel said.
>
> "No-one fights about this place – we have a nice road," Harry said.
>
> So the RCMP left.
>
> Everyone laughed. They laughed when he came out of the closet with his nose broken.
>
> Later he and Harry tried to glue his teeth but it didn't work. (116)

Though such humour is generally too leavened with sympathy to come at the characters' expense, some, like George Terri in *Lives*, are to a degree satirically presented, as is Antony in *Evening Snow*, who curries favour with inflammatory confirmations of gossip about his son Ivan's abuse of his girlfriend: "He slaps the snot out of her and everything else like that there . . . And she as pregnant as a butterball" (38). The satire in Richards' work, however, is largely reserved for the middle class, particularly those characters inclined towards "the affectation of concern" (as Richards puts it) such as Devoda Terri, who gossips about her concern for her socially deprived relatives to her "bridge-club composed of managerial wives in northern BC – who would above all talk about nasty little ploys and how to prepare trout cheeks" (*Lives* 278-79). Richards clearly sides with those at the receiving end of such condescension – for instance when he has Clinton Dulse, exasperated by the puritanism and intransigence of the principal and teacher who have expelled his son William for fighting, burst out, "If there was a whole nest of whores outside . . . neither one of you'd know how to catch the clap" (*Winter* 95). This side of Richards' writing has become more pronounced in his recent work, with the exposure of the self-aggrandizing and ultimately destructive social interventions of characters like Ruby Madgill and Vera Pillar playing a fairly central role in the Miramichi trilogy, and the satire of the academic Christopher Wheem being an important part of the recent *Hope in the Desperate Hour.* And, to Richards' credit, these relatively antagonistic characters are treated with a degree of sympathy too, even if the satire is sometimes over the top – when Armand Savard's daughter poops herself at a recital in *Evening Snow*, for example, "they did all the things other middle class families did. They got her to a psychiatrist, in Moncton, three times a month" (147). That the protagonists of these later works lean more towards the stoic than the picaresque, reflects the degree to which Richards takes such an opposition seriously.

This more polemical and orchestrated satire of the middle class is, I think, tied to the by-now-typical portrait of Richards' work as dour, depressing, etc. Richards has expressed again and again in inter-

views his objections to earnest, middle-class, sociological responses to his characters (and, having written a thesis in just this vein, I number myself among
the guilty). For various reasons, including the per-
ception of Richards as a voice for the Maritimes and
for the downtrodden, readers want to take
Richards' work too earnestly; the frameworks in
which Richards is usually viewed by critics and
reviewers – as social realist, as regionalist, as voice
for the working class – tend to impose a Vera-like
seriousness and solemnity and to obscure the fact
that there's much that's funny and heartening in the
lives of his characters. And such earnestness, especially of a socially conscientious sort, is not something that Richards views particularly favourably,
judging by how it fares in his fiction – and lately it's
been faring more and more.

Believe it or not: David Adams Richards is a
funny writer. And, I'm tempted to add, if readers
stop taking his work so seriously, maybe his carica-
tures of social concern in characters like Vera and
Ruby will be replaced with the warmer humour of
his earlier novels.

WORKS CITED

New, W. H. *A History of Canadian Literature*. Houndsmills, Hampsh.:
    Macmillan, 1989.
Richards, David Adams. *Blood Ties*. Ottawa: Oberon 1976.
——. *The Coming of Winter*. Ottawa: Oberon, 1974.
——. *Evening Snow Will Bring Such Peace*. Toronto: McClelland & Stewart,
    1990.

——. *Hope in theDesperate Hour.* Toronto: McClelland & Stewart, 1996.

——. *Lives of Short Duration* Ottawa: Oberon, 1981.

——. *Nights Below Station Street.* Toronto: McClelland & Stewart,1988.

——. *Road to the Stilt House.* Ottawa: Oberon, 1985.

Already Blessed

PAMELA JO BOGGS

Having been raised in poverty, I became a student at Hollins College somewhat apprehensively, unsure of the proper behaviours and etiquette of the educated upper classes. I was determined, however, to participate in writing courses, so I cautiously presented myself at an annual literary festival at the College. The first activity on the agenda was an opportunity to meet and receive an autograph from the authors attending. Upon entering the room, my breath became shallow as I viewed the large group of people in expensive looking clothing gathered there. Uncomfortably, I approached each writer and humbly asked for an autograph, moving quickly from one person to the next. By the end of the exercise I lacked but a single inscription, that of David Adams Richards, the Writer-in-Residence.

When I finally reached Richards, I instantly knew why he was difficult to find in the crowd. He had on a pair of blue jeans and a sweatshirt, and his signature was offered with as much resignation as it was asked for. Though we didn't speak, I sensed camaraderie from him, feeling him to be an honest man, rising above the pretense around us and simply enduring a consequence of his life's work.

After some time, the second half of the literary festival commenced, during which each writer read aloud from his work. Eventually, David Richards was introduced to read. As I listened carefully, I began to remember something I experienced while growing up. When I was a child in the coal mining territory of southwestern Virginia, my family only said grace over turkey and ham; that is, we only gave thanks to the Lord at Thanksgiving, Christmas, and Easter. I suppose beans weren't worth acknowledging, and, as for the game my father hunted, well, he'd say, "The thankin' was done when the guttin' was done," meaning that the food had already been blessed or else it wouldn't be on the table. Admittedly, this confused me for some time, and I was only really able to understand my father's informal benediction when I realized that he shared the same expression as Dave Richards when Richards finished reading that day. It was as if blood had spilled from Richards' words as it had from my father's game, and that neither man wanted to credit himself for what animal or mankind had suffered for those who would be nourished. As I look back on it now, the divine purpose is so evident that not giving verbal thanks is but the rejection of meaningless ceremony – and also the acceptance that such a gratitude is as insincere as a shallow "amen" from hungry bodies or a polite applause from a seemingly sophisticated audience.

There is a difference between having to hunt

and wanting to. The same is true for writing. A wise man is grateful for the strength it takes to endure every step of what God has put in his way to do, whether it be quietly abiding the brutality of gutting a deer in order to feed a family, or having to search the spirit and conscience of the poor to offer not only validation to them, but an understanding to those who are ignorant of their lives.

I know Dave now; he is a friend. Always was, though I just didn't know it because I hadn't read any of his books until I met him. The important thing I learned about proper behaviours and etiquette that day was that the only thing it takes to get it right is honesty, humility, and compassion. And if people are going to be offended by you, make sure the offense is rooted in your straightforward embrace of uncomfortable or unfashionable truths.

Learning About
the Crucifixion

The Religious Vision of For Those Who Hunt the
Wounded Down

J. RUSSELL PERKIN

I will begin with an admission. When I reviewed
David Adams Richards' *Evening Snow Will Bring
Such Peace* for the *Atlantic Provinces Book Review*
in 1991, I did not respond very positively to the
novel. It seemed to me a polemic against certain
commonly held liberal opinions, as though Richards
were digressing from his novel to make editorial
comments. However, when I read the final volume
of the trilogy, *For Those Who Hunt the Wounded
Down* (1993), I was struck by a different aspect of
Richards' novelistic technique: the prevalence of
religious allusions and the use of Christian narrative
structures in the novel. When I had occasion to re-
read *Evening Snow* almost seven years after my
review of it, the polemical passages I had previously objected to seemed to be far more integral to the
novel's world view than I had realized. Undoubt-
edly I have changed as a reader in seven years, but
the last novel of Richards' trilogy had taught me
something about how to read the preceding vol-
umes.

David Adams Richards poses something of a problem to the university-dominated literary establishment of Canada, which tends to be leftist in politics, and liberal, secular, and pluralist on ethical and social questions. On the one hand, Richards should be an appealing figure, for he writes about a region of the country which is "marginal," to use the fashionable critical term, and he often writes about characters who are poor or working-class. On the other hand, he has provided some fairly unflattering representations of liberalism and feminism, and he is preoccupied with the theme of individual moral integrity. In a critical climate dominated by postmodernism and political criticism, novels with epigraphs from Tolstoy and St. Paul are likely to be regarded as irrelevant if not embarrassing. One way of dealing with this embarrassment has been to describe Richards as a "regionalist," a label he rejects. As he told one interviewer:

> there is a real problem with critics because they're not saying what really annoys them . . . What bothers them is that I firmly believe that the only way a person can be free is thorough [*sic*] self- sacrifice. The only way a person can get something is to give something. But that's not the sort of standard progressive social milieu that we're all in, and if they read carefully enough they see this, and I think it bothers them and they say "this guy must be a Maritime regionalist, because his people think so differently." (*Studies in Canadian Literature* 160 [15 1990])

Here Richards implies that what critics object to is the fact that the world-view of his novels is fundamentally a religious one. His characters inhabit a fictional world in which there are identifiable ethical categories of right and wrong, good and evil, and the characters are seen to make meaningful choices within that world. In *Wounded*, for example, Nevin White is haunted by memories of his past behaviour, "Because he had not been kind, when some law greater than his required him to be" (116).

To a very significant extent, Canadian intellectual life has been formed by religious conviction (in particular by Catholicism and by social-gospel Methodism), and yet such conviction is often viewed with suspicion and disdain in intellectual circles today. I think this is one reason for the awkwardness which often characterizes the reception of Richards' fiction. A novelist who uses traditional religious discourse in a manner which is not overtly satirical or parodic is unlikely to find friends in the resolutely secular world of the contemporary university.

In a somewhat disdainful critical analysis of his earlier work, Janice Kulyk Keefer describes the world of *Lives of Short Duration* as "one in which traditional social structures have rotted away, with not a moral or cultural touchstone left in sight" (172). It would be difficult to make this comment

about Richards' later fiction, which is better
described by a comment of Eric Trethewey, who
writes that "like Dostoevsky and Flannery
O'Connor," Richards "has chosen to present his
vision through the traditional symbology of religious expression" (124). Trethewey's comment res-
onates with my own awareness of Richards' use of
biblical allusions and religious motifs in *For Those
Who Hunt the Wounded Down*, which is, in its shift-
ing perspective and representation of the effects of
ideological conflict in the lived reality of everyday
experience, a Dostoevskyan novel.

Far from being an exercise in minimalism or
dirty realism, the story of Jerry Bines takes a dangerous and unsuccessful man's life and invests it
with mythic qualities, while the continuation of the
story of Nevin White narrates the redemption and
rehabilitation of a character who sometimes seemed
the focus of authorial scorn in his previous appear-
ances in the trilogy. The more overt use of a
Christian pattern of redemption and of sacrificial
death in *Wounded* brings the religious concerns of
the previous two novels to the surface. *Wounded* is
also a departure in its narrative technique, for while
it has a Christian structure it is dialogical in a specific technical sense: much of the narrative is fil-
tered through the voice of the unnamed "man" who
is telling the story of Jerry Bines to a boy called
Andrew, and the climactic scene is presented
through a summary of Loretta Bines' testimony to

the police. This is something which is missed by Christopher Armstrong and Herb Wyile in the most extensive critical discussion of the trilogy to date. They state that "Richards's critique of progressive thought, particularly as represented by Vera, is consistently overdetermined in the interventions of the narrative voice of the three novels" (13). However, the narrative voice of *Wounded* is quite different from that employed in the two earlier novels; in fact, there is not a single clearly identifiable narrative voice. Similarly, the layering of time is far more complex than the relatively linear narratives of the first two works.

Richards uses the different voices in his novel to present a number of different versions of Jerry's life. To Andrew he is a romantic figure; to the men of the town someone to be both feared and respected; to Adele Pillar he is both the man who betrayed her father and the little boy she cared for as a girl. The version of Jerry which is treated most negatively is that of the social worker Vera Pillar, whose interest in Jerry is as a type of a certain mode of behaviour she is studying. Andrew's naive and sometimes romanticized view of Jerry's life has more in common with the implied authorial view than does Vera's. The narrator comments:

> All of her life Vera had gone from one religion to another asserting herself as its principal devotee. All his life Bines was searching for some notion of God, without ever having a concept of why he was. (183)

Andrew tries to understand Jerry with a different kind of language from Vera's, the imagery he has learned in his catechism class:

> He too was an orphan, in a way – like Bines was – but how different their lives. Learning his catechism at Sunday school, and learning about the crucifixion, he was told that each drop of blood Christ had shed was shed for a particular sin. This perhaps exaggerated claim was now manifested in the boy's psyche when he thought of Bines . . . (10)

Andrew is preoccupied with how much blood Christ would have to shed for the sins of Jerry Bines, but a series of allusions and events in the novel suggest that Jerry's death is itself a sacrifice on behalf of his family and his friends, whom he is trying to protect from the escaped killer Gary Percy Rils, who eventually murders Jerry in the presence of his ex-wife and son. This suggestion is reinforced by Ralphie Pillar's meditation on vicarious suffering:

> Once you yourself began to suffer you wanted the suffering to stop, and you would allow someone else to take it and bear it for you. (That this was the parable of Christ made no serious impact on Ralphie, who disliked religion.) (84)

Another wounded man in Richards' novel is the alcoholic Nevin White, a man haunted by a sense of his own personal failure, especially in the way that he treated his first wife. His path towards redemption takes him back to Fredericton, where he lived as a student, to ask forgiveness of her. Towards the end of the novel we see him as one of a gathering of Pentecostals who are raising a cross on their new church. The Pentecostal ministers are no saints; they are exploitative in their treatment of their flock, notably of Bines' ex-wife Loretta, but they nevertheless promise Nevin a new life, which gives him a reason to hope. And there, for Nevin, the novel ends, with an image of possibility.

Curiously, though Richards uses a number of biblical allusions in the novel and ends Nevin's story with the overtly symbolic act of raising the cross, the only direct quotation from the Bible is not accurate. In one scene, Jerry asks Loretta to read to him from the Bible, and she reads, "I am the true vine – and my Father is the husbandman; no one comes to the Father except by me" (137). When I went to track this down I discovered what one of my students was able to tell me without the help of a concordance: it is a conflation of two verses from different chapters of John's Gospel (John 15:1; John 14:6). Perhaps Richards was quoting from memory; perhaps Loretta is reading a text printed on a bookmark instead of reading from the Bible itself. The inaccuracy is a small point, but it does perhaps suggest that Richards is not concerned with a scrupulous fidelity to the Biblical text so much as with evoking the spirit of its meaning, that he is using the paradigms and imagery of Christianity in the name of a humanism which overlaps with religion, in opposition to a dogmatic social-scientific world-view. This may seem a large generalization to result from a small textual detail, but my conclusion also derives from my overall sense of the novel, which certainly does not ask the reader to endorse the truth claims of Christianity. Andrew remembers learning about the crucifixion, and he uses that knowledge to interpret the story of Jerry Bines, but he does not get a very satisfactory answer from his priest when he asks a question about the redemptive power of the Precious Blood (163). The image of blood being shed recurs not only in the fatal stabbing of Jerry, but in the scene of the raising of the cross, when Nevin scrapes the skin off his knuckles helping to lift it. However, as though Richards wanted to draw back from too obviously redemptive and Christian an ending, he then moves forward in time, providing a series of vignettes of the future of various characters, including the death of Lucy in a car accident. As a result, the conclusion of the novel suggests the randomness of everyday existence, as the story overflows the patterns which have been created by the man's, and Andrew's, and Richards' narration of Jerry's life. If, then, *For Those Who Hunt the Wounded Down* is a Christian novel, it is certainly one written for a post-Christian age.

WORKS CITED

Armstrong, Christopher and Herb Wyile. "Firing the Regional Can(n)on: Liberal Pluralism, Social Agency, and David Adams Richards's Miramichi Trilogy." *Studies in Canadian Literature / Études en littérature canadienne* 22.1 (1997): 1-18.

Keefer, Janice Kulyk. *Under Eastern Eyes: A Critical Reading of Maritime Fiction.* Toronto: U of Toronto P, 1987.

Trethewey, Eric. "The Moral Imagination of David Adams Richards." Rev. of *Hope in the Desperate Hour. The Fiddlehead* 193 (Autumn 1997): 121-26.

A Letter to a Friend

WAYNE JOHNSTON

I met Dave Richards in 1983 in his first year as Writer-in-Residence at the University of New Brunswick. I was a graduate student, taking a course in fiction writing from Bill Bauer who invited Dave to visit his class.

I had heard of Dave Richards before coming to UNB, but I had not read his books. All I knew of him was that some readers said they detected in his work the influence of William Faulkner and compared his fictional Miramichi region with Faulkner's Yoknapatawpha County.

Dave came into class that day carrying a Styrofoam cup which I presumed contained coffee. In fact, it contained nothing. It would, by slow degrees throughout his reading, fill up with spit from the plug of tobacco that he had wedged between his jawbone and his teeth. He paused while he read, and without a trace of self-consciousness or even a hint that this was not a standard practice among visitors to creative writing classes, spat and spewed tobacco juice into the cup. I remember looking around the class to see how the others were reacting. No one seemed to want to be the first person to let on that they did not know that this was what readers of fiction did while pausing between paragraphs.

He read from the book of his that is still my favourite, *Lives of Short Duration*. He read mesmerizingly, as I had never heard anyone read before. Those who have heard him read know exactly what I mean. It is impossible to describe to anyone who has not heard him read what it was like. He read with great conviction, and his unstinting, unqualified love for every one of his characters came through in every line.

It was not then fashionable to love your characters. It still isn't, I suppose. Certainly, it was and is unheard of to love *all* of them. There was the sense in his voice and in the sentences that I was hearing for the first time that he considered everyone to be caught up in the same joyful and ridiculous predicament.

He read the section from *Lives* about Little Simon and Blinkie, who were so often seen together that there was a rhyme about them. Blinkie could not sleep, so bothered was he by the sound of a cricket, which he swore was coming from behind the immovable fridge. To mollify Blinkie, Little Simon went in search of the cricket, even though he couldn't hear it. It was one of the funniest set pieces I had ever heard, so I was mystified as to why almost no one else in the class was laughing. Perhaps they all knew what was coming: Blinkie's death and Little Simon, while in mid-air, clicking his heels, seeing Blinkie on the undertaker's cutting board. As the passage moved from tender comedy to sorrow, the cadence of Dave's voice did not change. The account of Little Simon and Blinkie's happiness and friendship read like an elegy, and in the account of their misfortune and Blinkie's death there was a wonderful, indefinable redemption.

Somewhere in the reading was this sentence: "The snow flurried darkly upon the pavement like some northern apparition." The hairs stood up on the back of my neck. I had seen snow do exactly that, had felt exactly upon seeing it do that as I felt now upon hearing Dave Richards read this sentence. Not since I was a child had a sentence in a book erased for me so completely the gap between mind and world, life and literature.

As I would come to realize, there was, as far as Dave is concerned, no such gap. Dave reads books as if they are letters from friends about people he has known forever. Or rather, the books he likes read as if they are letters from friends about people he has known forever. If he does not like a book, it is because he does not think it does what a letter to a friend should do. It does not tell what the letter writer believes to be the truth.

Dave and I became friends, but not because, or at least not just because, we liked each other's work.

Since meeting Dave, I have discovered that a disconcertingly large number of people not only like but seem to understand the sport of curling.

That there are few things more enjoyable than to watch a truly awful movie with someone whose appreciation of cinematic wretchedness is even greater than your own. That if you are invited to the summer cottage of a friend, you may be assigned a bed whose mattress is dented down the middle as if, merely to accommodate you, your host has gone to the considerable pains of removing from it the anvil it contained for twenty years. That a friend should not be taken seriously the first five-hundred-and-seventy-three times he tells you he is moving to Toronto. I have discovered how wrong I was when I was twenty-four and believed that close friendships would be easy to come by.

It is not very often that you can point to a moment in your life and say that there, exactly there, something happened that changed you forever, something after which your life was never quite the same again.

I can think of three or four such times, and meeting Dave Richards that fall night in Bill Bauer's class was one of them.

Richards Demonized

The Academy as Greenpeace

LAWRENCE MATHEWS

Unlike some of the contributors to this special issue, I have no personal association with David Adams Richards. To say that it is as an academic that I have written about his work is to arouse instant suspicion that I may be an unwelcome guest here, since Richards' animosity towards academe is well-documented. But what I want to do is consider whether such animosity may be justified, using as evidence two different but in an odd sense complementary published critical discussions, one a recent article on the Miramichi trilogy by two young scholars, the other an analysis of *Nights Below Station Street* by a major figure in the Canadian academic world.

I'll begin by presenting an image drawn from the recent political history of my own adopted province, Newfoundland: Greenpeace versus the seal hunt. In this unequal struggle for public opinion, Greenpeace presents itself as certain of its moral and intellectual superiority. Its cosmopolitan suaveness enables it to control the agenda of the media, which routinely characterize the sealers as inarticulate, benighted, pursuing an archaic way of life. Greenpeace, you will have guessed, is the academy and Richards the sealer.

If this image seems extreme, consider the most recently published article on Richards, Christopher Armstrong and Herb Wyile's "Firing the Regional Can(n)on: Liberal Pluralism, Social Agency and David Adams Richards's Miramichi Trilogy." The issue, for them, is one of Truth (on their side) and Error (that, they regretfully conclude, would be Richards'):

> . . . Richards's trilogy appears set on revaluing the keywords of a largely discredited humanism – dignity, self-reliance, self-sacrifice, and moral action – an apparently regressive project . . . (15)

> Richards's didactic universalism and the valorization of "life" and realist aesthetics need to be challenged . . . (17)

> . . . it is hard not to lament the direction Richards's writing has taken – that is, the increasing tendency of the Miramichi trilogy towards didacticism and closure . . . (17)

Armstrong and Wyile's stated intent is to defend Richards, but in a way that underscores the patronizing nature of their approach; the last quoted sentence continues: "it is important to recognize that development as in part a response to the way Richards has been positioned in a cultural economy stratified particularly in terms of region and class . . ." (17). In other words, Armstrong and Wyile suggest that Richards' philosophical position is not the result of decades of intense thinking and feeling about art and life but rather something like a reflex action, a "response" to the way he has been "positioned," much as a lab rat reacts to an electric shock. (Sealers, from the point of view of Greenpeace, aren't evil – they simply don't realize how anachronistic they are.)

Armstrong and Wyile base their position on assumptions whose validity is so obvious (to them) that they need not be argued for. If we discard the academic words such as "largely" and "apparently," we find that the following propositions may be taken as axioms. Humanism is "discredited." Writing which affirms the contrary is "regressive." We all agree about "what needs to be challenged." Didacticism is bad. Closure is bad. These truths are self-evident. As Greenpeace preaches to the converted in its anti-sealing campaigns ("Citizens of Toronto, New York, London, send in your cash; show those uncivilized wretches who's boss"), so Armstrong and Wyile know how to work their common-room audience.

Where do they get this stuff?

Perhaps no one has been as indefatigable in his efforts to "discredit humanism" in the Canadian academic context as Frank Davey, whose reading of *Nights Below Station Street* is published with the chapter title "Maritime Powerlessness" in his *Post-*

National Arguments: The Politics of the Anglophone-Canadian Novel Since 1967 (1993). Let him represent the generation of scholars which has provided the intellectual mother's milk for the younger scholars like Armstrong and Wyile. (One index of the chapter's representational quality is that it was first published in a journal edited by Davey himself.) Davey's discussion is striking in its attempt to demonize Richards – and through him an unidentified but evidently broad range of "recent discourses of Atlantic Canada" (79) – as being in thrall to outdated "pastoral ideologies" (78).

In order to effect such demonization, Davey adopts an interpretive stance located at that point at infinity at which theoretical sophistication and will-ful obtuseness converge. I can't address all of the points that his discussion raises; I'll concentrate on his comments on the novel's ending, with which I assume readers of this collection will already be familiar. Davey's premise is this: what happens to the characters is to be understood simplistically in terms of propositions about what happens in life. Because the novel ends with a series of "life-affir-mative results" for characters who have not strug-gled to achieve them, Davey concludes that "the book's characters . . . are construed by this narrator and novelist as better off leading passive, acquies-cent, non-constructive, geographically limited lives, rather than ones of ambition and effort" (78). Is it possible, one wonders, that Richards may have had some other artistic purpose than to advance in fictional form a crude argument about the futility of "ambition and effort"? Not as far as Davey is concerned. He accuses Richards of treating his characters with "condescension" (78), apparently blind to the irony that such a word could be used to describe his own attitude to Richards.

An alternate reading would involve the hypothesis that *Nights Below Station Street* occurs in a fictional world designed to function according to the conventions of parable, that indeed it embodies what Armstrong and Wyile call a "tendency . . . towards didacticism and closure" (17), though its point escapes Davey – from whose Gradgrindian perspective there *should* have been a lesson, and it should have included a thesis about the importance of "education, technology, the desire for literary production or even for self-improvement" (78). ("Atlantic Canadians, pull yourselves up by your bootstraps!") But perhaps Richards is attempting to address readers of – to put it kindly – a slightly different cast of imagination than Davey. Perhaps Richards arranges for "life-affirmative results" to flow from "chance events" not because he naively believes that in life such things are likely to happen but because, in the case of the characters concerned, they *should*. That is, the cluster of events at the end of the novel emphasizes the narrative's implicit evaluation of the characters' moral and spiritual condition.

Resolutely ignoring this possibility, Davey notes that Joe Walsh and Allain Garret, the characters who "perform rescues in the concluding chapter" are associated with "hunting, woodlore and subsistence farming" while the two "endangered characters" (Vye and Myhrra) are identified with "urban culture and its reliance on advanced technology" (76). To understand the ending of *Nights Below Station Street* in these terms is to interpret the parable of the Good Samaritan as an impassioned plea for better policing and emergency medical services on the road from Jerusalem to Jericho. Vye and Myhrra have throughout the novel been associated with an inauthenticity on a personal level that far outweighs any last-minute focus on their connection with "urban culture" and "advanced technology." (Doesn't Joe live in the same community and drive a truck?) True, Vye and Myhrra are not at home in the woods as Joe and Allain are – but this fact has parabolic significance as an index of their spiritual status.

Joe Walsh is the character who, in his novel-long battle against alcoholism, has done more than any other to enact Armstrong and Wyile's unholy quaternity of discredited humanism ("dignity, self-reliance, self-sacrifice, and moral action"). The novel's concluding sequence reveals Joe most fully as the embodiment of the spiritual power that animates such virtues, as (despite his chronic back pain) he carries Vye out of the woods, "not knowing the processes of how this had all happened, only understanding that it was irrevocable because it had" (225).

For Davey, this sentence is the last in a series of narratorial comments on "the inadvertence of the character's actions" (76). For less hostile readers, it might be a comment on the sense of mystery that accompanies such moments of grace. But to be such a reader, one must (a) be willing to entertain the seriousness of such notions as "grace" and (b) be willing to entertain the possibility that, despite any differences in class, economic status, province of residence, and intellectual ability, the humanity of Joe Walsh is not inferior to one's own.

But to speak in these terms is, to revert to the Greenpeace image, to define Richards as the sealer. After all, to write about grace and mystery is as anachronistic as to kill seals for a living. In Ontario there are abattoirs where animals are dispatched in a civilized manner, and the people who live there have outgrown the need for grace and mystery, thank you. Political and economic power will suffice.

And with that power comes the Greenpeace-like self-assurance to pronounce on the failings of others. How regrettable are those "problematic recent discourses of Atlantic Canada"! (79). Amusingly, Davey presents as one of his examples "the Newfoundland government that reconstructs and opposes the Meech Lake Accord as something done to Newfoundland rather than negotiated by it" (79) – as bizarrely misleading a half-sentence as could be written on the subject.

I began by raising the question of whether Richards' animosity toward academe is justified. Yes, it is.

Davey, Armstrong, and Wyile represent the mentality currently in control of the literary element of Canadian academic institutions. It is a mentality that sees itself as in some way superior to that which produces the art that was once its object of study. It gets things backwards. Richards does the cause of literature a service when he complains about this, whether in interviews, essays, or (most heinous of literary crimes!) in his novels themselves.

WORKS CITED

Armstrong, Christopher and Herb Wyile. "Firing the Regional Can(n)on: Liberal Pluralism, Social Agency, and David Adams Richards's Miramichi Trilogy." *Studies in Canadian Literature / Études en littérature canadienne* 22.1 (1997): 1-18.

Davey, Frank. *Post-National Arguments: The Politics of the Anglophone-Canadian Novel Since 1967.* Toronto: University of Toronto Press, 1993.

Richards, David Adams. *Nights Below Station Street.* Toronto: McClelland & Stewart, 1988.

The Beginnings of a Literary Friendship

ERIC TRETHEWEY

I first encountered David Adams Richards in the autumn of 1983. I had returned to Canada, after a fifteen-year exile, to teach in the English Department at the University of New Brunswick. As luck would have it, David Richards was the Writer-in-Residence that year. I had made two earlier attempts to come home to the Maritimes, but neither had worked out. And though in 1983 I was more determined than ever to make a go of it in Canada, ultimately I was not offered the tenure-track position I had hoped for. Now, when I look back over that dark year, the brightest aspect was my friendship with Dave Richards.

I had read some of Dave's work before meeting him. In *The Coming of Winter*, *Blood Ties*, and *Lives of Short Duration* I encountered powerful, incantatory verbal portraits of aspects of Maritime life that unfolded with the shock of recognition. He was writing about a world I knew intimately, had inhabited throughout my childhood and youth. I was enthralled. Northrop Frye and others have remarked that it is only when a culture becomes sophisticated that it can afford to become more regional – that it can accept its own reality as being a worthwhile thing in itself rather than as being a pale, imperfect shadow of some distant, more authentic reality. For me, Dave's fiction represented that stage in Maritime letters – it was a regionally stamped literature that was not self-conscious but that presented itself unabashedly as art with universal claims.

From the very beginning of my experience at UNB, it was clear that I was not to be embraced as returning prodigal. Rather, I was for the most part treated as a rank outsider, a native Maritimer doubly marginalized. I recall the then poetry editor of *The Fiddlehead* – a magazine in which I had published poems, stories, and essays over the years – remarking to me that he was editing an anthology of poetry from Atlantic Canada. When I asked him if he would consider a submission from me, he demurred, pointing out that I had been here only a short time. Apparently, being born in a place and spending twenty-something years coming of age there counted somewhat less than being a landed immigrant from the U.S.A. or the U.K. Shortly after this incident, a graduate student rejected a group of my poems on the grounds that they were "too traditional," by which I assumed that he meant they made sense. Though there were a few individuals at UNB who treated me decently, at least on the personal level, these two incidents were typical of the year I spent there.

If it had not been for David Richards – the friendship he proffered, the passionate talk about literature, the moral support he gave to my own writing – I would have spent a very isolated, discouraging year of a homecoming that was not.

The first time we conversed was late in September at a reception hosted by the President of the University. We talked about boxing, to begin with, I suppose because Dave had heard I had been a prizefighter. Right away, it was evident that we had a common interest in the sport. He mentioned a fighter from Nova Scotia I had gone to high school with, Stu Gray, who had since died. Years before, Stu had fought the main event at the Halifax Forum the night I fought, in a prelim on the same card, my second professional fight. From then on, Dave and I were on the best of terms.

Soon, he began inviting me to his home in Fredericton and we began to talk about literature, discovering in each other lifelong omnivorous readers who loved and admired many of the same writers: The great Russian novelists of the nineteenth century; the English Romantic poets, John Keats in particular; William Faulkner; and Maritime writers such as Alden Nowlan and Alistair MacLeod. We also agreed on a mutual distaste for the pretensions of the international *avant-garde* who in the interests of "making it new" had been doing the same sort of trifling song-and-dance routine since the 1890s. Again and again, our talk turned to the ways in

which literature represented the moral underpin-
nings, or lack thereof, of human relationships: love,
justice, compassion, egotism, greed, thoughtlessness,
cruelty. I discovered that Dave had a deep understanding of and profound repugnance for cruelty.

One night at his home we talked about
Dostoyevsky's novel *The Possessed.* At the time
there seemed to be an uncanny echo of its concerns
in the culture around us. There was a kind of callow
liberalism/progressivism in the air, a complex of
ideas and attitudes purely notional and not second-
ed by conduct or rooted in any real self-knowledge
or insight into human nature. It was as though
many, particularly in the universities, thought they
could don an ideology, like some fashionable gar-
ment, and suddenly be made whole and *au courant.*
Both of us felt the hollowness of this phenomenon,
and Dave's way of resisting it was to write a
sequence of great novels informed by a deeply poetic, profoundly moral sensibility rooted in a self-
knowledge that came from the experience of mar-
ginality, cruelty, and, yes, even degradation. His
compassion has never been a thing of the surface. It
is interesting for me now to think of connections
between the literary life at UNB that year, the intellectual circle around Stepan Verkhovensky in *The
Possessed,* and the group of writers/intellectuals in
Dave's novel *Hope in the Desperate Hour.*

Around the middle of October that year we
both began to participate in regular writing work-

shops held in the old Ice House on campus. I knew
from conversations with Dave that the Ice House
Gang had been supportive of and helpful to him
when he was first starting out as a young writer. But
the personalities had changed in the group, apparently, because some of the present members seemed
driven by personal agendas and egotism rather than
a genuine concern to see the thing in itself as it really was, to use an Arnoldian locution. Here, for
example, is an exchange that, in exasperation, I
recorded at the time:

N: You used a lot of "which" clauses in those
stories.

K: Yes, I did, but it was really just an affectation
on my part since Fulford [the editor of *Saturday
Night*] changed these all to "that," which is proper
in the first place.

Dave has a terrific sense of humour, but trifling
such as this is funny only on stage, not in real life.
Inoculated, perhaps, against this sort of thing
because of my more extensive experience of academic life, I stayed with the group for the remain-
der of the academic year. Dave, however, dropped
out after a couple of times. In the wake of such driv-
el, it was not difficult to imagine why.

From the beginning of our relationship, Dave
struck me as not being quite at ease in the academic world. At first I did not understand why, since his
extensive reading, his love of literary conversation,
and his passionate love for books ought to have

made him feel at home. At the time, I still believed, in spite of abundant evidence to the contrary, in the university as an ideal spiritual and intellectual community where minds could meet in a context of openness and generosity and compassion. Those values, at least, were shared by both of us. But I suspect Dave saw way back then that given human nature and the arrogance attendant in privilege and power that institutions of higher learning were more likely to be characterized by posturing and empty rhetoric – places where vanity permitted personal peculiarities and sometimes downright irresponsibility and weirdness to be raised to intellectual principles.

As I indicated in the beginning, the job at UNB did not continue and I ended back in the U.S.A., this time in all likelihood for good. But my long-time friendship with Dave Richards has been a true homecoming in its own right. And every time I read a new book of his, or re-read an old one, I'm once again back in a Maritimes of the imagination, hearing the speech, seeing the landscape, and experiencing that realm of true art where people I recognize love and suffer and die in the context of a real world constructed out of a genuine writer's talent and care.

On Staying the Course

ALISTAIR MACLEOD

I first heard David Adams Richards read on August 20, 1980. There was a large crowd in the auditorium at Mount Saint Vincent University in Halifax and I recall the evening as being very warm. Most of the people in the audience were members of the Canadian Council of Teachers of English and they were holding their annual conference in the Maritimes; Halifax to be specific.

On the stage there were three metal chairs occupied by Alden Nowlan, David Adams Richards, and myself. We were there to represent, in our different ways, I suppose, "the literature of the region." Years earlier when I was a student at the University of New Brunswick Alden Nowlan had written me a very warm and encouraging letter from Hartland, N.B. He had read some of my work in student publications. I was very much in awe of Nowlan at the time I received the letter because I was then a "student" writer and considered myself to be "young." At the time of the letter's reception David Adams Richards was eleven years old. By 1980, though, Alden Nowlan had already befriended and encouraged David Adams Richards and *Blood Ties* bore the simple dedication "For Alden Nowlan."

On the evening of the reading, Alden Nowlan seemed very composed and David Adams Richards very shy and I imagine myself as being somewhere in between. I mention this memory because it has to do with what time does to all of us.

Today David Adams Richards is, arguably, the best novelist practicing his craft in Canada. If time is gentle to him he may one day win the Nobel Prize for Literature. He is *that* good! He has produced a body of work exceptional in both quality and quantity and at the centre of his work is an understanding of the human heart possessed by relatively few of his contemporary writers. He is careful and protective of this human heart that has been entrusted to his care yet he is also tough and brave enough to ensure its fierce safekeeping. Like so many of his characters, he is capable of the winter journey through knee-deep snow cradling within him the talisman of his love. He is indeed a writer who can withstand external storms and he will not melt beneath the rain. It is good that he is so.

Today, in spite of the deserved praise that has come his way, there still exists a school of criticism that is sometimes antagonistic towards his work. This may be partially due to the fact that in this age of "core and periphery," Richards consistently deals with characters who live their lives on the so-called "edge" – geographically, socially, culturally, and perhaps even linguistically. It is worthwhile to realize that it has nearly always been thus and strong writers from the designated "regions" have always found a certain kind of "attitude" when judged by those who see themselves as occupying the urban/critical centre. If time is kind and truth is free, in the end, of course, it does not matter. Life is short while art endures.

Shortly before his death, George Ryga said to me, "All of the best literature comes from all of the worst places." I did not realize that George Ryga was so close to his own death at the time and that I would never have a chance to speak to him again but I have thought about him and his statement quite frequently throughout the intervening years. I certainly do not believe that the Miramichi is one of "the worst places." Indeed, it may be one of the very best. But it is interesting to remember that the very urban Henry James once dismissed the great Dorset writer as "Poor little Thomas Hardy" and that the elitist Virginia Woolf once said that the early writing of James Joyce reminded her of a young undergraduate scratching his pimples. It is a good thing, for all of us, that Thomas Hardy and James Joyce did not take these statements to heart and stop writing.

In the eyes of literary London, D.H. Lawrence came from an unfashionable place and so did Emily Brontë. *All* of Ireland was considered unfashionable in the century previous to ours and perhaps that prejudice/attitude continues to exist. But what of the literature itself?

I have spent most of my life teaching literature
to relatively young people. I think of my students as
"the people" and I try, in my work, to teach the literature as literature and to avoid dispensing "attitudes" towards that literature. I have found that students love to discuss *Wuthering Heights* or *The
Mayor of Casterbridge* or *Frankenstein* (written by a
nineteen-year-old who was the subject of much criticism during her young life) or *The Sound and the
Fury* (rising out of that most maligned state of
Mississippi). They never ask if these novels may
have come "from the worst places" of their time.
But they do know that these novels come from and
speak to the human heart. These novels have, as
they say, "the power" and the power is almost tan-
gible as it reaches out to them across geographical
and generational lines. It may well be that human
nature does not change very much and is as enduring as the art it seeks to find.

At this period in time when David Adams Richards
reads, there is a general silence in the room.
Sometimes, if it is dark, the audience cannot be seen
and there is only a small light illuminating the reader and his page. Sometimes, part way through the
reading, one can feel the audience reacting. One can
feel, as well as hear, people caught in the grip of
their own tears. This is, I suppose, what Keats called
"synaesthesia" – the blending of more than one

sense within a single image. Sometimes Richards himself has almost to stop as if he finds it difficult to continue. This is because his work contains an emotional quotient that is, at times, almost impossible to bear. This is the power of the word – rising from the small illuminated page and going out to the people who wait within the darkness. This is the power of great art – to show us to ourselves and make us better through its medium.

It is, perhaps, difficult to predict the future artistic output of David Adams Richards. Perhaps he will write "the great Toronto novel" (the much-discussed "presence of an absence") but, suffice to say, that "the great Miramichi novel" has already been written and, consider also, that there is more than one.

"Love is not love / Which alters when it alteration finds," Shakespeare tells us, but rather "it is an ever-fixed mark / That looks on tempests and is never shaken." We wish the mariner, David Adams Richards, continued constancy in his ability "to stay the course" – for himself and for us and for all the cargo of his care.

Biographical Note

TONY TREMBLAY

Born in Newcastle, New Brunswick in 1950, David Adams Richards is a novelist, poet, playwright, screenwriter, essayist, and short story writer. His first volume, *Small Heroics* (1972), is a collection of poems that chart the imagined landscape of his subsequent work. In 1974, *The Coming of Winter*, his first novel, was published, followed by *Blood Ties* (1976) and *Lives of Short Duration* (1981). Together with a collection of short stories, *Dancers at Night* (1978), these first three novels form a trilogy that traces the intersecting lives of working-class characters.

In 1986, he received a short-listing for the Governor-General's Award for *Road to the Stilt House* (1985), and the Canadian Book Information Centre's award as "One of Canada's Ten Best Fiction Writers." In 1988, the first book of Richards' second trilogy, *Nights Below Station Street*, appeared, winning the Governor-General's Award. Two other major awards followed (the Canadian Authors Association Award and the Canada-Australia Literary Prize) for the second novel in the trilogy, *Evening Snow Will Bring Such Peace* (1990). In 1993, the final novel in the second trilogy, *For Those Who Hunt the Wounded Down* was released, and similarly acclaimed, winning the

Atlantic Provinces Booksellers Award and the Thomas Raddall Award. Two of the three novels in the second trilogy (*Nights* and *Wounded*) have been translated into screenplays by Richards and made into films, and Richards' original screenplay, *Small Gifts* (1994), has also aired several times on CBC TV. In addition to the many prizes and awards he has won for fiction, Richards' screenplays have also been recognized. He has won Gemini Awards for Best Writing and, in 1996, won the coveted New York International Film Festival Award for Best Script for *Small Gifts*.

Forays into the essay during the mid 1980s, which Richards published as *A Lad From Brantford & other essays* (1994), led him to write two book-length non-fictional accounts about hockey and fly-fishing: *Hockey Dreams: Memories of a Man Who Couldn't Play* (1996) and *Lines on the Water: A Fisherman's Life on the Miramichi* (1998), which won him a second Governor-General's Award, making him only the third writer in Canada to win a GG in two categories. In his last three novels – *Hope in the Desperate Hour* (1996), *The Bay of Love and Sorrows* (1998), and the Giller-Prize winning *Mercy Among the Children* (2000) – Richards continues his exploration into the valour and complexity of the human spirit. His latest novel, *River of the Broken Hearted*, appeared in 2003.

Richards currently lives in Toronto with his wife Peg and their two sons, John Thomas and Anton.

Bibliography

PRIMARY SOURCES (SELECTED)

Richards, David Adams. *Small Heroics.* Fredericton: New Brunswick Chapbooks # 17, 1972. (Poems.)

——. *The Coming of Winter.* Ottawa: Oberon Press, 1974.

——. *The Dungarvon Whopper.* 1975. (Stage play.)

——. *Blood Ties.* Ottawa: Oberon Press, 1976.

——. *Dancers at Night.* Ottawa: Oberon Press, 1978. (Short stories.)

——. *Lives of Short Duration.* Ottawa: Oberon Press, 1981.

——. *Water Carrier, Bones and Earls.* 1983. (Stage play.)

——. *Road to the Stilt House.* Ottawa: Oberon Press, 1985.

——. *Tuesday. Wednesday.* 1987. (Original screenplay.)

——. *Nights Below Station Street.* Toronto: McClelland & Stewart, 1988.

——. *Evening Snow Will Bring Such Peace.* Toronto: McClelland & Stewart, 1990.

——. Adapted Screenplay for *Nights Below Station Street*, 1990/1998.

——. *For Those Who Hunt the Wounded Down.* Toronto: McClelland & Stewart, 1993.

——. *Small Gifts.* 1994. (Original screenplay.)

——. *A Lad from Brantford & other essays.* Fredericton: Broken Jaw Press, 1994.

——. *Hope in the Desperate Hour.* Toronto: McClelland and Stewart, 1996.

——. Adapted screenplay of *For Those Who Hunt the Wounded Down.* 1996.

——. *Hockey Dreams: Memories of a Man Who Couldn't Play.* Toronto: Doubleday Canada, 1996.

——. *Lines on the Water: A Fisherman's Life on the Miramichi.* Toronto: Doubleday Canada, 1998.

——. *The Bay of Love and Sorrows.* Toronto: McClelland & Stewart, 1998.

——. *Mercy Among the Children.* Toronto: Doubleday Canada, 2000.

—— . Adapted screenplay of *The Bay of Love and Sorrows.* 2002.

——. *River of the Broken Hearted.* Toronto: Doubleday Canada, 2003.

SECONDARY SOURCES (SELECTED)

Armstrong, Christopher and Herb Wyile. "Firing the Regional Can(n)on: Liberal Pluralism, Social Agency, and David Adams Richards's Miramichi Trilogy." *Studies in Canadian Literature / Études en littérature canadienne* 22.1 (1997): 1-18.

Connor, William. "The Unlikely Heroes of David Adams Richards' Second Trilogy." *International Fiction Review* 25. 1-2 (1998): 71-77.

——. "A Controlled Poetic Nationalism." Rev. of *Road to the Stilt House. The Fiddlehead* 147 (Spring 1986): 107-109.

——. "The River in the Blood: Escape and Entrapment in the Fiction of David Adams Richards." *World Literature Written in English* 26 (Autumn 1986): 69-77.

——. "Coming of Winter, Coming of Age: The Autumnal Vision of David Adams Richards' First Novel." *Studies in Canadian Literature* 9.1 (1984): 31-40.

——. "A Note on George Byrne's Argument that Orville is the Central Character in *Blood Ties*." *Studies in Canadian Literature* 8.1 (1983): 142-148.

Currie, Sheldon. "David Adams Richards: The People on the

Roadway." *The Antigonish Review* 99 (Autumn 1994): 67-75.

——. Rev. of *Nights Below Station Street*. *The Antigonish Review* 73 (Spring 1988): 65-68. Rpt. in *Contemporary Literary Criticism*, No.59.

Mathews, Lawrence. "Revenge of the Swedes." Rev. of *A Lad from Brantford & other essays*. *Essays on Canadian Writing* 61 (1997): 71-74.

——. "David Adams Richards and His Works." *Canadian Writers and Their Works* (Fiction, Volume 12). Eds. Robert Lecker, Jack David, Ellen Quigley. Toronto: ECW Press, 1995.

Perkin, J. Russell. "Moralizing on the Miramichi." Rev. of *Evening Snow Will Bring Such Peace*. *The Atlantic Provinces Book Review* (Feb.-Mar. 1991): 11.

Sterrer-Hauzenberger, Inge. "'OIGOA/Sepoitit – You Are Beautiful': Narrative Technique and Major Themes in Two Novels by David Adams Richards: *Lives of Short Duration* and *Road to the Stilt House*." Unpublished M.A. Thesis. University of Vienna, 1989.

Tremblay, Tony. "Answering the Critics: David Adams Richards and the Paradox of Unpolularity." *The Antigonish Review* 128 (Winter 2002): 119-28.

——. "David Adams Richards: Canada's Independent Intellectual." *The Hollins Critic* 36.4 (October 1999): 1-14.

——. "David Adams Richards." *Encyclopedia of Literature in Canada*. New, W. H., Ed. Toronto: University of Toronto Press, 2002. 966-68.

——. "Television, Book Reviewing, Hockey, Don Cherry, and David Adams Richards – on navigating the differences between politics and culture." *Pottersfield Portfolio* 18.1 (Fall 1997): 119-23.

——. "Hockey & other things." Review Essay of David

Adams Richards' *A Lad From Brantford & other essays.* *Pottersfield Portfolio* 17.1 (Fall 1996): 83-85.

——. "An Unblinking Eye on Passion and Triumph." David Adams Richards' *Hope in the Desperate Hour.* *The New Brunswick Reader* 3.23 (April 1996): 20-21.

——. "David Adams Richards: An Appreciation." *BRICK: a literary journal* 51 (1995): 30-32.

——. "Road From the Stilt House." Review of David Adams Richards' *For Those Who Hunt the Wounded Down.* *The Fiddlehead* 180 (1994): 116-20.

Trethewey, Eric. "The Moral Imagination of David Adams Richards." Rev. of *Hope in the Desperate Hour.* *The Fiddlehead* 193 (Autumn 1997): 121-26.

Wheaton, Margo. "Largely a Matter of Perspective: The Role of the Individual, the Social and the Universal in the Social Vision of David Adams Richards." Unpublished B.A. Thesis. Mount Allison University, 1987.

Wyile, Herb. "Taking the Real Home to Read." *Open Letter* 7/6 (1989): 5-16.

——. 'Now You Might Feel Some Discomfort': Regional Disparities and Atlantic Regionalism in the Writings of David Adams Richards." Unpublished M.A. Thesis. McGill University, 1986.

Contributors

A native of southwestern Virginia, Pamela Jo Boggs studied writing at Hollins College when David Adams Richards was Writer-in-Residence there.

Fred Cogswell, a key figure in Canadian literature for the last half century, has been writing poems for the past 66 years. His latest collection, *Ghosts*, was released in 2002.

William Connor is a member of the English Department at the University of Alberta. Since 1991 he has served as Associate Dean of Arts and, currently, Dean of Students. He is writing a book on aspects of David Richards' fictional world.

Sheldon Currie is from Reserve Mines, Cape Breton, N.S.. He is a retired professor of English from St. Francis Xavier University in Antigonish, N.S., and is the author of the best-selling novel *The Glace Bay Miners' Museum* (1996), and the short story collection *The Story So Far ...* (1997).

Wayne Curtis is a novelist and a short story writer who is from the Miramichi but who now lives in Fredericton. His recent books include the acclaimed novel *Last Stand* (1999) and the short fiction collections *Preferred Lies* (1998) and *River Stories* (2000).

Born in St. John's, Newfoundland, Wayne Johnston received an M.A. in English from UNB in 1984. His first book, *The Story of Bobby O'Malley* (1985), won the W.H.Smith/Books in Canada First Novel Award. His latest books include the novel *The Colony of Unrequited Dreams* (1998), the fictional memoir *Baltimore's Mansion* (1999) and the novel *The Navigator of New York* (2002).

Frances MacDonald lives in Fredericton.

One of Canada's most accomplished short story writers, Alistair MacLeod is the author of *The Lost Salt Gift of Blood* (1976), *As Birds Bring Forth the Sun and Other Stories* (1986), and the acclaimed novel *No Great Mischief* (1999), which won the International IMPAC Dublin Literary Award.

Lawrence Mathews teaches at Memorial University of Newfoundland. He has published a monograph on David Adams Richards in the ECW Press series *Canadian Writers and Their Works* (1995).

J. Russell Perkin teaches English at Saint Mary's University in Halifax. He is particularly interested in the relationship between religion and literature.

New Brunswick's foremost English-language writer, David Adams Richards has put the Miramichi region on the world's literary map. A writer of poetry, short fiction, screenplays, nonfiction, essays and polemics, Richards' most prodigious work thus far has been as a novelist. His eleventh novel, *River of the Broken Hearted*, was published in 2003.

Inge Sterrer-Hauzenberger was born in Upper Austria in 1963, studied English and German literature and linguistics at the University of Vienna, and graduated in 1989 with a Diplomarbeit (M.A. Thesis). She lives in Austria with her husband and children.

Tony Tremblay teaches Canadian literature and Cultural Studies at St. Thomas University in Fredericton, N.B.. He has written about Richards since 1986, and is currently completing the critical biography of Richards.

Eric Trethewey is the author of several collections of poetry, the latest of which are *Heart's Hornbook* (2003) and the forthcoming *Songs and Lamentations* (2004). He teaches English at Hollins College in Virginia.

Margo Wheaton lives in Halifax and received her M.A. in English at Dalhousie University. Her poetry and reviews have appeared in *The Fiddlehead*, *Room of One's Own*, *Contemporary Verse II*, *Pottersfield Portfolio*, and *The Coast*.

Herb Wyile teaches Canadian Literature in the Department of English at Acadia University. He is the author of *Speculative Fictions: Contemporary Canadian Novelists and the Writing of History* (McGill-Queens 2002) and co-edited two special journal issues, *PastMatters: History and Canadian Fiction* and *A Sense of Place: Reevaluating Regionalism in Canadian and American Writing*.

Printed in May 2005
at Gauvin Press Ltd., Gatineau, Québec